MEET KATHARINE DREXEL

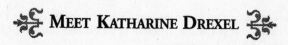

Meet Katharine Drexel

Heiress and God's Servant of the Oppressed

Mary van Balen Holt

CHARIS

SERVANT PUBLICATIONS
ANN ARBOR, MICHIGAN

Charis Books is an imprint of Servant Publications especially designed to serve Roman Catholics.

Servant Publications—Mission Statement
We are dedicated to publishing books that spread the gospel of Jesus Christ, help Christians to live in accordance with that gospel, promote renewal in the church, and bear witness to Christian unity.

Scripture verses are from the Revised Standard Version of the Bible, copyright 1946, 1952, 1971 by the Division of Christian Education of the National Council of Churches of Christ in the U.S.A. Used by permission.

Servant Publications
P.O. Box 8617
Ann Arbor, MI 48107
www.servantpub.com

Cover design by Paul Higdon, Minneapolis, Minn.
Cover photo: Sisters of the Blessed Sacrament, Bensalem, Penn. Used by permission.

02 03 04 05 10 9 8 7 6 5 4 3 2 1

Printed in the United States of America
ISBN 1-56955-313-0

Library of Congress Cataloging-in-Publication Data

Holt, Mary van Balen.
    Meet Katharine Drexel : heiress and God's servant of the oppressed / Mary van Balen Holt.
        p. cm.
    Includes bibliographical references.
    ISBN 1-56955-313-0 (alk. paper)
        1. Drexel, Katharine Mary, Saint, 1858-1955. 2. Christian saints–United States–Biography.   I. Title.
    BX4700.D77H65 2002
    271'.97–dc21
    [B]

                                                                          2002008777

❦ DEDICATION ❦

*To the Sisters of the Blessed Sacrament, and all people
who respond with God's love and wisdom to the challenges
of faith and social justice in the world today*

CONTENTS

❧ ACKNOWLEDGMENTS ❧

Information from varied sources and the input of many people have helped bring this book to completion. First, I drew heavily on two previous works that detailed Katharine Drexel's life. Especially for information about her family, and their early life together, I used *The Francis A. Drexel Family*, written by Sr. Dolores Letterhouse, S.B.S., at the request of St. Katharine's sister, Louise Drexel Morrell. This book is full of charming, vivid anecdotes and letters.

I also owe a debt of gratitude to Sr. Consuela Marie Duffy, S.B.S., who wrote the definitive work *Katharine Drexel: A Biography*. In addition to presenting the broad scope of her life's work, this book includes excerpts from St. Katharine's correspondence with her two spiritual directors, giving the reader a glimpse into the heart and soul of Katharine Drexel. I have quoted liberally from both sources and used their material throughout this book. They provide informative reading for one interested in learning more about St. Katharine.

Unable to list all the people who assisted in this project, I will recognize as many as space allows. Most importantly, I thank the knowledgeable and gracious archivist at the motherhouse of the Sisters of the Blessed Sacrament, Stephanie Morris, Ph.D., C.A. She cheerfully opened the doors (and boxes) of the archives to me, even when blizzards threatened, locating materials I asked for as well as materials I did not know enough to request, but which brought the saint to life. St. Katharine left thousands of written documents, and Dr. Morris works untiringly to make them accessible. In addition to hours in the archives, she was available by phone and email to answer questions I had forgotten to ask.

The Sisters of the Blessed Sacrament at their motherhouse in Bensalem, Pennsylvania, welcomed me into their lives for two weeks, giving me a quiet place to work, pray, and be renewed. They willingly shared stories of St. Katharine and their own interesting lives spent working in missions across the country. Sr. Thomasita Daley and Sr. Ruth Catherine Spain, who worked long on the canonization process; Sr. Inez Carney, formerly Mother Katharine's nurse; and Sr. Roberta Smith, a postulant when St. Katharine was still active, are just some of the sisters who gave of their time. Sr. Jean Ryan and Sr. Patricia Marshall spoke to me of possibilities for future action of the order and its social justice ministry. Sr. Beatrice Jeffries, Vice President, S.B.S., outlined the present state of the order and its missions. Though not all these sisters are quoted in this book, their insights and information helped form a foundation for writing.

My editor, Paul Thigpen, and others at Servant have assisted in bringing this book to completion. To these and to the others I do not have space to list, I give my sincerest thanks. If any mistakes or inaccuracies appear, the fault is mine alone.

❧ INTRODUCTION ❧

St. Katharine Drexel's riches-to-rags story turns conventional wisdom upside down. Why would an heiress of millions of dollars leave a life of luxury for one of poverty and service? Hers was a life of contrasts. She crossed the ocean on luxury liners and traveled backwaters of the Louisiana bayou in a rickety launch; she was as familiar with Harlem streets as she was with those of Paris. On various occasions in her long life she dined in elegance with the elite of high society and in simplicity with Lakota chief Red Cloud and his wife.

An adventurous woman, Katharine traveled the West when railroads stopped in Omaha and buckboard wagons and horses' backs were the only way to get to the mission. She and the sisters of her order stood their ground when vandals smashed windows and set fire to a barn. Ku Klux Klan threats of bombing did not drive them away.

Renouncing wealth is a compelling story, but St. Katharine's life is more than an example of material generosity. She speaks to those jaded by a materialistic world with her gift of self. The words of Cardinal Dennis Dougherty, written for her jubilee celebration, are as appropriate for Christians today as they were for those who heard them in 1941: "If she had never done anything else than set such an example to a frivolous, self-seeking world, she should be regarded as a benefactress of the human race. She gave her immense fortune to her work. She did still more by giving herself to it."[1]

What motivates such sacrifice? Near the end of her life, St. Katharine wrote, "Love! Love! Let us give ourselves to real pure love.... The renewal which I seek and which we all seek is a work of love and can be accomplished by love alone."[2] Hers is a story of passionate love that speaks to hearts weary of the world's empty promises, and it will stir its readers with a desire to participate in that love themselves.

ONE

Roots

Every family is unique, offering various kinds of nourishment and challenges to its members. While each child's genetic code dictates to some extent physical appearance, intellectual ability, and artistic gifts, his or her family exerts profound influence. Some families are like rich, loamy soil, bursting with nourishment and promise. Others are like clay, reluctantly giving what little sustenance lies hidden beneath a hard surface.

St. Katharine Drexel was in part the fruit of her lineage. As her story unfolds, the importance of family and its influence is evident. Katharine's ancestors contributed their richness to the soil where she would sink her roots.

Grandfather Drexel

Francis Martin Drexel, Katharine's paternal grandfather, was born on April 1, 1792, in Dornbirn, Austria. Though his father was a merchant, Francis dreamed of becoming an artist. His childhood and young adult years were lived amidst the turmoil of the Napoleonic wars. After receiving some formal education, eleven-year-old Francis studied in Italy for nearly a year. He returned home and later, following his natural interest, was apprenticed to a painter.

In 1809 his father sent him out of the country to avoid conscription into the enemy's army. Francis wandered through Europe, painting portraits. He briefly visited home in 1812, but returned to his itinerant ways, again avoiding service in the French army. When peace was restored in 1815, he came home, but before long decided to seek his fortune abroad, joining hundreds of others who were setting off for America.

Arriving in Philadelphia in 1817, Francis opened a portrait studio and taught at Bazeley's Female Seminary. During this time he met Anthony Hookey, a grocer, and was particularly attracted to his daughter, Catherine. She and Francis were married at St. Mary's Catholic Church on April 23, 1821.

Together, Francis and Catherine had six children: Mary Johanna; Francis Anthony, who would become Katharine's father; Anthony Joseph; Joseph Wilhelm; Heloise; and Caroline. The couple's life together was punctuated by the elder Francis' travels. When his portrait business and teaching position came to an end as a result of unfounded scandal, he left his family for South America. He traveled there, painting portraits and sending money home. In 1830 he returned to Philadelphia, but left again in 1835 for Mexico and Central America.

The Banking Business

During the financial crisis in the United States precipitated in part by Andrew Jackson's opposition to the National Bank, the elder Francis returned and opened a small broker's office in Kentucky. He was successful and relocated to Philadelphia. Soon his two oldest sons were helping him.

Starting with tasks such as working at the counter and serving as night watchman, fourteen-year-old Francis Anthony began to learn the banking business. He earned extra money by making time for another lifelong passion: music. On Sundays he walked six miles each way to play the organ at St. John's Church.

The Drexel banking establishment flourished, and when the gold rush hit, the elder Francis turned Drexel & Company over to his sons and went west. There he founded another company, Drexel, Sather & Church. He returned to Philadelphia in 1857, but his untimely death in a train station accident in 1863 left his sons at the helm of the growing financial empire.

Joseph joined his older brothers and was sent abroad to form yet another branch of the growing Drexel business: Drexel, Harjes & Company. Soon another banking house was founded in New York: Drexel, Morgan & Company. Francis Anthony and his brothers managed the business well and eventually made the fortune that would be shared with a variety of charitable organizations through the generosity of the Drexel family.

Hannah Langstroth

Little is known about Katharine Drexel's mother, Hannah Langstroth Drexel. She was the fourth and youngest child of Piscator and Eliza Lehman Langstroth, born at Greenwood farm near Philadelphia on January 14, 1826. Her family was of German stock and had arrived in the United States with early settlers of the Pennsylvania colony. Hannah shared her parents' Anabaptist faith, belonging to a sect known as the Dunkards.

Francis A. Drexel married Hannah on September 28, 1854, and soon after, on August 27, 1855, their first child was born: Elizabeth Langstroth Drexel. Three years later, on November 26, 1858, they had a second daughter, Catherine[1] Mary Drexel, named after her paternal grandmother. In giving the world a precious new life, Hannah sacrificed her own. Five weeks after giving birth, on December 30, she succumbed to complications of childbirth and died.

In a response to a letter of sympathy received from a cousin, Francis shared not only his grief but also the comfort afforded by his faith:

> I am again alone in the world with two children, the youngest five weeks old—my bereavement, though very afflicting, lately had not been unexpected. After three weeks intense suffering, although she may have been unconscious of it, having lost her reason, my beloved one was taken from me. If I know myself I am resigned to this dispensation of the Almighty. His will in all things be done, for He ordereth all things wisely and well.... I have every assurance that my beloved one has gone to her heavenly Father.[2]

So, early in life, Katharine was wrapped in the loving arms of her large, extended family, an embrace she and her sisters would know many times. Her Aunt Ellen and Uncle Anthony Drexel drew the young girls into their home and cared for them for two years until Francis remarried.

The Bouviers

On April 10, 1860, Francis wed Emma Bouvier in St. Joseph's Catholic Church in Philadelphia. Emma was one of eight children of Michel Bouvier and Louise Vernou. Michel was an emotional Frenchman who could angrily spout English at his hapless countrymen when travel plans went awry, or shed tears over a revisited battlefield while his even-tempered wife provided balance.

Emma's siblings became part of the Drexels' extended family. One of her sisters, Louise, became a member of the Religious of the Sacred Heart, the same order that ran academies in Philadelphia where the Bouvier girls had been educated. Emma and Madame Louise remained particularly close, so Louise proved to be influential in the Drexel girls' lives.

TWO

Early Years

After a six-month honeymoon trip through Europe, Francis and Emma Drexel returned to their home at 1503 Walnut Street in Philadelphia. Elizabeth and Katharine were reunited with their father and new mother, who loved them as dearly as she would later love her own daughter.

Katharine now had three sets of grandparents, something she wondered about as a child and came to understand at the age of thirteen when she discovered Emma Drexel was not her biological mother. These families provided sound nurture for the Drexel children.

Family, the First "Sacrament"

For ten years, the Drexels lived on Walnut Street during the winter and rented a summer residence in rural Nicetown, Pennsylvania, affectionately calling it "the nest." Mornings during those summer years were pleasant, filled with family breakfasts and time to frolic in the yard and barn. Sometimes the two sisters were allowed to drive a small donkey cart to visit Grandma Langstroth in Germantown, or to shop at the local store for necessities. As if driving one's own donkey cart were not reward enough, the girls bought ginger cookies and munched them on the way home.

When Francis returned from work each day, he, Emma, and the children often took a carriage ride before supper. After enjoying some family time the girls were readied for bed, but before sleeping they rejoined their parents for a rosary and night prayers.

Soon, Elizabeth and Katharine made room for a third member of the family. Louise Bouvier Drexel, nicknamed "angel's gift," was born on the feast of the Guardian Angels, October 2, 1863. Even in childhood Katharine and her little sister shared a special bond. All three girls were devoted to one another, growing up in a home filled with love where no thought was given to their being born of different mothers.

With the birth of Louise came another addition to the Drexel home, Johanna Ryan. Johanna had entered the convent of the Sacred Heart, but her health was not suited to the demands of religious life. So she was sent by Aunt Louise to the Bouvier home to work. When Emma's baby arrived, Grandma Bouvier sent Johanna to help with the children. Johanna became a beloved companion who remained with the Drexels until her death in 1906.

From the start, Emma Drexel made sure Katharine and Elizabeth retained ties with their mother's family. They visited Grandma Langstroth every Saturday. Dressed in the traditional plain Dunkard garb, Grandma Langstroth may have appeared stern, but she knew young children and what they needed, which was love most of all. She had a playroom filled with toys and books, and the young cousins spent hours there. Outdoors they had a pond stocked with goldfish, an arbor, and plenty of space in which to play.

These childhood days were filled with experiences that made wonderful stories in later years. One that brought a smile to Mother Katharine's face in the retelling was her account of how Elizabeth once blurted out that Grandma Langstroth would not be going to heaven. When asked why, the girl recounted what she had learned from zealous but misinformed Johanna: Only Catholics could go to heaven! Needless to say, Grandma was upset, but a few conversations with

Frank and Emma straightened out the matter.

Once, while walking home from the Langstroths' house, Katie fell into a frog-filled pond. Drenched and covered with muck and slime, she was returned to the Langstroths, where she was bathed and dressed in Grandma's clothes until her mother sent clean ones from home.

The children learned the lessons that country living has to teach. Time surrounded by God's creation in rural Philadelphia may have helped young Kate develop her appreciative and keen eye. Later, as an adult traveling across the country, she drank in landscapes and vividly described them in letters written home.

The girls visited their Drexel and Bouvier grandparents as well. When Emma took her daughters to visit Grandma Bouvier during the week, she knew her sister would be there as well with her own children in tow. The cousins played while their mothers visited with Grandma, a stately and proper matron, receiving visitors in the library as if they were royalty. Grandma and Grandpa Bouvier were then visited again each Sunday morning.

On Sunday afternoons, Johanna took the girls to visit Grandma Drexel, who had cookies and fruit on hand for young visitors. This home, too, was often filled with relatives. Here is where Katharine met Uncle John Lankenau, who came to hold a special place in her heart.

Both John and Mary Drexel Lankenau gave generously to charities. John succeeded Grandpa Drexel in his work with the local German hospital, later becoming president of that institution, which eventually bore his name. After his wife died, in her memory John built a home for the aged and brought Lutheran sisters from Germany to staff it. Eventually his plans expanded to include a school for girls, a mother-house for the deaconesses, and a children's hospital. When he died, he left large sums of money for each of his three Drexel nieces' charities, including Katharine's new order.

What is most striking about Katharine's large extended family is not its wealth, though surely that had an effect on her. Money could and did provide security, excellent education, and opportunities available only to the privileged. However, most important was the love and warmth they freely shared with one another.

As we have seen, Katharine's family tree was peopled with engaging characters: an excitable French grandfather who made fine furniture; his wife, an aristocratic Philadelphian of unflappable personality; an Austrian grandfather who was an itinerate portrait painter turned banker; a grandmother who must have been patient to raise her family so often alone; an Anabaptist grandmother who provided her grand-children with a well-stocked playroom in which to spend their winter visits; and rafts of cousins, aunts, and uncles. The overall picture is one of loving nurture and support. Anyone who has had the experience of spending days romping with cousins or talking with a favorite aunt or uncle can imagine the experience of Katharine's childhood days.

Family is the first "sacrament." In it one experiences God through flesh-and-blood faces, arms, and hearts. When a mother holds a cry-ing infant close, the child experiences God's loving embrace. When a father reassures a young one who is afraid of a storm, the child knows the safety of God's love. Such experiences give human beings some way to understand the love of God with us.

Katharine once related one of her earliest memories that illustrates this truth. One day when she was very young, her family went to the beach. The little girl was petrified by the waves pounding at the shore. The rest of her family plunged into the water, but Katharine stayed back.

Suddenly her father returned to her and swung her up onto his shoulders. He walked into the surf, and Katharine clung to him for dear life:

There I was pick-a-back, my little arms hugged tight around my father's neck. The salt spray splashed into my face, papa ducked, and I was under the water, he met a great wave which dashed against and then over us—frightened beyond words I held on like grim death feeling my only safety was in my father's arms. He brought me back to the shore, my fear gone. Many times in after life that incident has given me courage for I felt my Heavenly Father's arms were protectingly around me as had been dear papa's.[1]

Katharine was blessed with a family whose faith, love, and joy in their children provided many human metaphors for the divine love she responded to in adult life. The Drexel family was not perfect, as no human family can be. But it was indeed rich soil. It is not surprising that God's call to holiness, sown in each one of us, found fertile ground in Katharine Drexel's soul.

"Prayer Was Like Breathing"

Prayer was woven into the life of the Drexel household. Emma set aside a special place in their Walnut Street home for her family members to spend special quiet time with God. Their oratory contained an altar, candles, a crucifix, and pictures and a bust of Our Lady.

When Francis returned from work, he preferred to spend a half hour praying on his knees in his own room. This conversation with God was often continued as Francis played the organ, letting it give voice to the prayer in his heart. Besides private prayers, the family prayed the rosary and night prayers together each day. They regularly attended Mass and received the sacraments of the Eucharist and Confession.

Mrs. Drexel often took the girls with her when she made visits to the chapel of the Sisters of the Sacred Heart. Children will be children, and the young Drexel sisters were not always pious, sometimes playing in the chapel. Still, they saw their mother make time in her day to spend with God present in the Blessed Sacrament. The importance of prayer and God's presence was not missed.

Katharine's capacity and desire for a relationship with God showed itself early in her life. Even as a child, Katie had a profound devotion to the Lord present in the Blessed Sacrament and longed to receive it, as these letters she wrote reveal:

This letter is not a bit like Lizzie's. I composed this one myself. You must not laugh, dear Mama, at my English letter to Saint Joseph; I really know how to spell now. Please keep all my French letters so you can see what progress I am making. Mama, I wrote this one all by myself. I am hoping Saint Joseph will make me speak French. Dear Mama, I am going to make my First Holy Communion and you will see how I shall try to be good. Let me make it in May, the most beautiful of all the months.

Good-bye now, I shall write you soon again.

KATIE DREXEL WHO LOVES YOU.[2]

I am going to make the Stations of the Cross for you, my darling Mama, and for Papa and Louise, too. I am trying to study hard so that I may make my First Communion this year.[3]

As it was, Katie did not make First Communion until she was eleven. She was prepared, as were her sisters, by the Sisters of the Sacred Heart convent. The day arrived on June 3, 1870.

Bishop James F. Wood celebrated Mass, gave Communion, and administered Confirmation. Mrs. Drexel had arranged a special breakfast for all the children, their mothers, and the archbishop. In a letter to her Aunt Louise, Katie recounted the morning's events. Though she wrote about the wonderful breakfast, she treasured the spiritual experience in her heart and would comment later, "Jesus made me shed my tears because of his greatness in stooping to me."[4]

Remembering the prayer life of her family, Mother Katharine Drexel later shared this account of her childhood years:

Prayer was like breathing ... there was no compulsion, no obligation ... it was natural to pray.... Night prayers were always said together. We were usually in bed by eight o'clock when we were children. Then in our little night-dresses we would go to the top of the stairs and call down, "Mama! Papa!"

Then Papa (we did not call him "Dad") would leave his organ or his paper and Mama her writing, and both at the call of the children would come up and kneel for night prayers in the little oratory. Sometimes, Mama would be sleepy ... yes, she would be worn out from her work with the poor ... and would doze off and say, "Hail Mary, Mother of God." No matter how often this would happen she would begin all over when Papa would gently say, "Dear, it is Holy Mary, now, Holy Mary, Mother of God ..." Yes, he knew she was tired after her day.[5]

The Drexel girls not only experienced a constant flow of personal and sacramental prayer in their lives; they witnessed prayer of action.

Emma Drexel spent much of her time and energy serving the poor in a work she called "Dorcas." Two or three days a week she opened her home to the needy of Philadelphia, enlisting the help of her daughters and encouraging them to contribute their own money to the effort.

Katharine, wondering whether the neighbors minded such a group gathering day after day, watched her mother distribute money, food, clothing, and whatever else was required. Emma was careful, keeping records of aid given and hiring a woman to check on the needs of those requesting help. Over $20,000 plus rent for 150 families passed through her hands each year.

Francis Drexel also set a fine example for his daughters. He was an active member of numerous charitable associations in Philadelphia, giving of his time as well as his money. Even Johanna and other family employees became involved in the family's charitable works. With such models, the sisters' later responses as adults to need and injustice were not a surprise. Elizabeth, Katharine, and Louise, each using their individual gifts and the inheritance that one day was theirs, continued to work for the poor and neglected.

Education

When time for Elizabeth's formal education arrived, she was sent to the school run by the Sacred Heart Sisters on Walnut Street. Later, the Drexel girls' education was centered at home. Emma hired tutors for music, Latin, and French, and "Miss Cassidy" to oversee the general instruction. A young Irish immigrant, Mary Ann Cassidy was recommended by Aunt Louise and became her students' lifelong friend and confidante. She was a true teacher who shared her own love of learning while delighting in that of her pupils.

To provide a place for study, Mrs. Drexel arranged a room in the house with "a bay-window, convenient map-rack, picture-covered walls, study-table, piled with interesting books, & its jardiniere of green ferns."[6] She had a natural sense of how to nurture children's inborn curiosity. Katharine retained her enthusiasm for learning throughout life, a tribute to her teachers and to her mother, who had the wisdom to educate her children in such a way.

As far as Miss Cassidy was concerned, composition was a cornerstone of education, providing instruction in language mechanics, communication skills, and handwriting. She had the girls writing letters to one another, to their parents, and to herself. Many of Katharine's childhood letters were saved and are in the archives at the motherhouse of her order.

Besides providing glimpses into a happy childhood, these youthful letters also reveal Katharine's spiritual side, seen in this letter written at age nine to her sister Louise:

Happy Birthday and many happy returns of birthdays as happy as these you have passed up to your seventh in our snug little nest. That the holy angels whose feast it is may ever bless and protect you and keep you as pure and as innocent as they are themselves in Heaven is the prayer of your lovingest

SISTER KATIE[7]

Geography and history were studied in part by family travel, and Miss Cassidy insisted upon the girls writing travel journals and letters home. Each time the family returned, she corrected the entries, and the students carefully recopied their writing. This letter reflects Katie's awareness not only of physical beauty around her but also of a deeper spiritual reality:

This evening I have consoled myself in taking a last look at the Glen, before our departure for Crawford House tomorrow. It is a scene which varies at every sunset. The mountains before us, Madison, Jefferson, Adams, Clay, Mt. W., and other surrounding peaks, can never be made soft and beautiful, however by any sunset. They can never melt into the heavens, like beautiful Jacob's ladders as some mountains do; but they remind one, in their might, bald grandeur, firmness, and solidity of eternity— the time that was, the time that will be.[8]

Anyone who has ever kept a notebook knows they open one's eyes to both the outside world and the world within. Some entries record natural surroundings or activities. Others capture thoughts and feelings. Sometimes writing becomes prayer, a conversation with God.

Katharine's notebooks must have done all these things for her. When she struggled to discern her vocation, she poured out her heart and soul on paper. Even in her later years, she kept notebooks and wrote thoughts and prayers on small scraps she saved from the wastebasket. Miss Cassidy's insistence on writing encouraged Katharine to use that valuable tool for her entire life, giving to those who came later a window into the mind and heart of a saint.

San Michel

In 1870, Mr. Drexel purchased a ninety-acre farm in Torresdale, Pennsylvania. When he remodeled the farmhouse, a stone carving of St. Michael was placed above its door, and a locally made stained-glass window depicting the saint was placed at the top of the first flight of stairs. The patron of Katharine's grandfather, Michel Bouvier,

St. Michael became the protector of their country home. Just as their first summer residence had been dubbed "the nest," this estate was called "San Michel" and was home not only to the Drexel family but also in later years to St. Katharine's religious family of nuns.

Besides fixing the home, Mr. Drexel had outbuildings, cottages for servants, and a greenhouse built on the property. He also put his mark on the farmland. Some was cultivated as pasture, while other parts were planted with new trees, shrubs, and flowers. He referred to it as "our picture gallery" and enjoyed walking through the grounds and gardens with his family.

The family took up residence there in June 1871. Each daughter had chores to do, and Katie's was overseeing general household operations. Not long after they had moved in, Mrs. Drexel suggested the girls run a Sunday school for children of employees.

Katie and Elizabeth did most of the work, with Katie teaching the younger children. The school, which ran through the summer, was popular and eventually had more than fifty students. Katharine later recalled: "Just before St. Michael's was closed for the winter, prizes were given out for the best lessons and best attendance, and on Christmas Day the children assembled for a celebration when they received useful gifts (such as dresses, knitted jackets, etc.) also cake, candy, etc. This Sunday School was held until 1888." [9]

During the family's years at San Michel, the small, rural church of St. Dominic's became the Drexels' parish. In 1872, Fr. James O'Connor was made its pastor. An Irishman who studied at a seminary in Philadelphia and then in Rome, he had been made rector of seminaries in Pittsburgh and Philadelphia. Having had some difficulties with the archbishop, he was removed from the seminary and sent to the little country parish. This move was providential for Katharine.

Fr. O'Connor often visited San Michel and developed a close

friendship with the family. Even though Katie was just fourteen when she moved there, she was already wrestling with her call, trying to understand and respond to the pull of God upon her heart and soul. Fr. O'Connor became her spiritual director from those days until the end of his life and was profoundly influential in her discernment of vocation.

Katharine lived in a world of wealth, filled with people of power, position, and connections. She moved through it with ease and yet, deep within, she was immersed in another, spiritual, world. Her notebooks allow us to look into her hidden life.

January 1, 1874—Another year has come around and I will renew my resolutions again for I am but little better. I was much better in May than I am now because I suppose I have relied too much on myself....

March, 1874—Next Wednesday will be Lent and so to please God and mortify my flesh, I resolve:
1. Not to eat between meals
2. Not to take water between meals
3. Dinner, everything but once
4. No butter, no fruit
5. To speak French
6. To give money to the poor.[10]

Katharine's notebook entries reveal a teenage girl striving to grow in holiness not by esoteric spiritual practices but by responding in her day-to-day life in a holy, self-sacrificing way. Speaking French, offering works to God upon hearing the clock chime, spending a little time to start the morning with prayer, reading lives of the saints or other good books, being kind and more patient, being disciplined in consumption of food, giving alms—such little ways to holiness are available to all. Small as they seem, they require discipline, perseverance, and divine help.

Who cannot see themselves in these comments from Katie's notebooks?

How many things in looking over my book I have commenced to do and then have not completed! [undated, 1876].[11]

Lent has commenced and still I am as bad as ever and perhaps worse. How is it possible I could treat Him so badly after all He has done for me? [February 2, 1878].[12]

May is not yet finished. I have put down the account and find that I have done scarcely anything to correct pride and vanity. I will try to be kind as that seems to be the virtue which makes us humble. I asked Jesus to give me the grace of kindness and maybe He will give it to me [May 1878].[13]

Despite inevitable failures, Katie prayerfully continued her efforts. She had not only the advice and encouragement of a spiritual director and confessor but also the example of a deeply Christian family whose faith informed every aspect of life.

Not all are called to embrace the vocation of life in a religious order, much less to found an order. But all are called to holiness. Katie's parents, sisters, and many in her extended family took that call seriously. Her slowly maturing vocation found nourishment in family and friends who surrounded her.

A Trip to Europe

In September 1874, the Drexel family and Johanna boarded the ship *Scotia* and set off for London. They spent almost six months visiting England, France, Germany, Switzerland, Austria, and Italy. Education was woven into their time abroad, and as always, the girls were expected to keep journals and write letters to Miss Cassidy.

Whether recounting the delights of sucking icicles and eating snow in Switzerland, or describing those she met while traveling, Katie's accounts were full of her usual enthusiasm for life. They also gave evidence of the sixteen-year-old's awareness of the spiritual journey.

We first wended our way towards the cathedral, the street leading to which, "by the by" reminds me of the road to heaven, for the path commences by being wide which may be interpreted as I supposed as the way of innocence which we traverse after baptism, & then narrows & becomes so crooked that only once & a while can the cathedral spire (heaven) be seen.[14]

That spiritual awareness may have broken into her consciousness at particular moments, or it may have been the reality that gave light to all she saw or heard. Everything she did, everyone she met, had the potential to help her experience the One who had created her and the world in which she lived. Either way, her writings leave no doubt that realities deeper than those apprehended by the senses filled her mind and heart.

God was moving deep within her. Her sense of his presence would grow throughout her long life, marking her as a natural contemplative whether she lived life busily in the world or, as she did in later years, confined to bed.

Katie was delighted to experience European cathedrals as a physical connection between the faithful of ages past and those of her own day, as she mentioned in this letter to Miss Cassidy after visiting the cathedral in Vienna:

We had a splendid opportunity of seeing the interior of the cathedral after Mass, & the beautiful stained glass of the sanctuary, the monuments, chapels, painting & statues were all thoroughly examined. I shall not attempt to tell you what an extremely vast place this cathedral is, for I never can describe well but all I shall say is, that there is to me such an attraction to these old Gothic churches in which the dust of ages is still lingering, that, although we have seen many cathedrals even more vast than this one, I never tire of looking at them & always leave them with regret.[15]

The family continued its trek through Western Europe. Christmas was pleasantly spent in Naples, but as Elizabeth remembered in a composition she wrote later, they were looking forward to the following year's holiday celebration at San Michel. When in Rome, the Drexels saw Pope Pius IX. After joking with Louise, who had offered him a new calotte placed carefully on a silver tray, the pontiff put his own cap on her head. The white cap became a treasured family keepsake.

Next the family entered France, where Katie was moved by her experience at the shrine in Lourdes. "I attributed to no superstition the spiritual refreshment that I drank from the clear fountain which she herself caused to flow and which has been the channel of so many wonderful blessings."[16]

Family roots drew the Drexels to Pont St. Esprit, hometown of Grandfather Bouvier. The sun shone as they walked through the village and attended Mass at the small church where their grandfather had prayed as a child. They spent a day being entertained and well fed by relatives, but left early the following morning. After six months, the Drexels were ready to return home, and by June they were back at San Michel.

❧ THREE ❧

Eventful Years

The years following the European tour were filled with life-changing events for the Drexels. In January of 1876, Kate's sister Elizabeth made her social debut. Also in 1876, Fr. O'Connor was made bishop and became the founding bishop of Omaha, shepherding Catholics not only in Nebraska but also in Wyoming and the Dakotas.

Distance did not weaken the close relationship that had been forged between the bishop and Katie. In the years that followed, she continued to depend on him for spiritual direction and encouragement. Their correspondence reveals O'Connor's loving guidance, vision, and humility as he came to recognize and support Katie's understanding of her call to religious life.

A Young Woman

In 1878, Kate finished her formal schooling. Her letter to Bishop O'Connor reflects feelings of ambivalence.

> This will be a perpetual vacation for me, and yet strange to say, I do not feel particularly hilarious at the prospect. One looks forward so many years to finishing school, and when at last the time comes, a kind of sadness steals over one whose cause is hard to analyze. Perhaps it comes from this—there was a definite future

to look to, up to the time of leaving school. Then the future suddenly looks all vague and uncertain.[1]

After her debut in 1879, which twenty-year-old Kate barely mentioned in her letters to Bishop O'Connor, he wrote two lovely letters to her from Omaha. In one he wondered how he should address the girl-turned-young-woman. In the other he affirmed the promise life held for her:

> You have indeed cleared "The Capes" and ... are now making trial trips along the coast and in the offing.... Your cargo is not all aboard, but even now how precious the freight you carry! The hopes and affections of a young heart, that until now has loved only God and what God loves. An immortal soul "purchased with a great price," virtuous habits formed by divine grace, and the action of the Holy Spirit, "the promise and the potency" of a large fortune to help the poor, to benefit religion, and, in so doing to thrice bless its possessor. The good example and the merit of a long life spent for God in a social station where He is but little thought of—these and other treasures are "between the decks" in "the Katie Drexel of Philadelphia." ... *Bon Voyage!* then to the Katie whithersoever her course may be, now or in the future.[2]

Kate and Elizabeth spent much time traveling to the seashore and visiting family and friends. During this time, the two Drexel daughters carried on correspondence with their parents. When Emma and Frank wrote to their daughters, they admonished them to enjoy themselves but to be cautious. Their father wrote: "I hope you are careful not to get into deep water either with the beaux or the surf."[3]

The year 1879 also brought hard times to the Drexels. Emma's health was failing. Attempting to shield her family from worry, she arranged to have an operation, not at a hospital as recommended by her doctor but at the family's Walnut Street home. Making an excuse, she drove into Philadelphia and underwent surgery, which revealed cancer.

Once Francis discovered his wife's condition, he engaged the best doctors to care for her and made a trip with her to Colorado, hoping the change would help her condition. It did not, and Emma's illness lingered for three pain-filled years. When she was well enough, Emma traveled with her family to places closer to home.

While in Sharon Springs, New York, in 1882, Louise, too, became seriously ill. This development added stress to the family, but as this letter to a close friend shows, Francis bore the suffering with deep faith:

God spared us trials for a very long time and we have been exempt from the common lot, and if in His mercy He sees fit to afflict us, we must endeavor to bear it and with resignation, knowing it is for our good. You have had severe and constant trials to bear and have always borne them uncomplainingly. My brother, too, has had a life of constant trial. Why should we complain?

Lizzie and Kate have been good and affectionate daughters and most efficient nurses. They take turns in attending. God has blessed us with the best of children.[4]

As Francis had written, Kate and Elizabeth cared for their mother throughout her illness. While she patiently bore her agonizing pain, Emma offered her pain as prayer that her husband could be spared when his time came.

All the love and attention of her family and doctors could not save Emma, who died on January 23, 1883. She was mourned not only by family and friends but also by countless others whom she had helped through Dorcas and her life of service. The editorial of *The Public Ledger*, February 2, 1883, recounted:

> The poor, the sick, the unemployed, the dying were the constant objects of her cheering visits. Few women ever secured so many situations for needy but industrious and worthy persons—men, women, boys, and girls. The families she has aided can be numbered by the hundreds, some of them supported entirely by her in time of need.[5]

Considering the Religious Life

If Emma's death brought sorrow to those she had helped, it brought unspeakable grief to her family. It inspired Elizabeth to continue her mother's work and to follow her path in the world. Seeing such intense suffering in one who had lived life trying always to be faithful impressed upon Kate the gravity of original sin, and she began to consider seriously a religious vocation.

At the suggestion of her confessor, she wrote out the pros and cons of such a move, and on May 21, 1883, sent them in a letter to Bishop O'Connor:

My Reasons for Entering Religion

1. Jesus Christ has given His life for me. It is but just that I should give Him mine. Now in religion we offer ourselves to God in a direct manner, whereas in the married state natural motives prompt us to sacrifice self.

2. We were created to love God. In religious life we return Our Lord love for love by a constant voluntary sacrifice of our feelings, our inclinations, our appetites. Against all of which nature powerfully rebels but it is by conquering the flesh that the soul lives.

3. I know in truth that the love of the most perfect creature is vain in comparison with Divine Love.

4. When all shadows shall have passed away I shall rejoice if I have given in life an entire heart to God.

5. In the religious life our Last End is kept continually before the mind.

6. A higher place in heaven is reserved for all eternity.

7. The attainment of perfection should be our chief employment in life. Our Lord has laid a price upon its acquirement when he says, "If thou *wilt* be perfect go sell what thou hast and give to the poor and thou shalt have treasure in heaven and come follow Me.... He that followeth me *walketh not in darkness.*" How can I doubt that these words are true wisdom, and if true wisdom why not act upon them?

My Objections to Entering Religion

1. How could I bear separation from my family? I who have never been away from home for more than two weeks: At the end of one week I have invariably felt "homesick."

2. I hate community life. I should think it maddening to come in constant contact with many different *old maidish* dispositions. I hate never to be alone.

3. I fear that I should murmur at the commands of my Superior and return a proud spirit to her reproofs.

4. Superiors are frequently selected on account of their holiness, *not* for ability. I should hate to owe submission to a woman whom I felt to be stupid, and whose orders showed her thorough want of judgment.

5. In the religious life how can spiritual dryness be endured?

6. I do not know how I could bear the privations and poverty of the religious life. I have never been deprived of luxuries. When with very slight variety the same things are exacted of me day in and day out, year in and year out, I fear weariness, disgust, and a want of *final* perseverance which might lead me to leave the convent, and what then!![6]

Kate confessed that in doing the exercise she had not come to any decision about her vocation but had made a novena and had sought the prayers of others. She also confided that she had received and turned down a proposal of marriage secret from all but her father. She trusted Bishop O'Connor with the deepest concerns of her heart and was sure that she could do no better than to rely on his guidance.

The bishop's response clearly showed that he was not impressed with her reasons for wanting to become a religious. He called them "impersonal, that is abstract and general," while responding to her personal reasons for not entering religious life one by one. Her abhorrence of community life he thought serious. All difficulties can and have been overcome by many, but not without the resolve "to endure them for Our Lord." [7]

Replying to Kate's next letter, Bishop O'Connor suggested some sacrifices she could make, such as eating less and skipping her favorite dishes, or dressing in clothes not the most becoming, to test her resolve. "Think, pray, wait," he counseled her. [8]

Those might not have been the words Kate wanted to hear, but she acted on his advice. Her desire was always to follow God's will, which she trusted was mediated through her spiritual advisor. "I fear to undertake anything," she wrote, "no matter how small it may be unless it is in conformity with the Divine Will, because God gives me the strength necessary to perform what He prompts; but if I follow the inspirations of pride He will not support me and I shall fail." [9]

Second Trip to Europe

While Katharine was occupied with spiritual concerns, her father was searching for a way to distract the family from their grief. He arranged a fall trip abroad for himself and his daughters. As with their previous trip, correspondence passed between the travelers and Miss Cassidy, who had been left behind to care for the home. Though Europe offered magnificent sights and pleasures, nothing was as compelling to Kate as the yearning in her soul to follow God's call and give herself completely to him.

In the letter she wrote to Bishop O'Connor while crossing the ocean on the *Scythia,* the profound influence of her mother's suffering and death is clear:

Since dear Mamma's rest in God I have felt no inclination to read novels. Perhaps I am wrong in indulging my feelings; but when dear Mamma went to our true home, I felt life to be too serious a passage into eternity to wish to spend my odd minutes in reading of the joys of this world. I believe I am partially afraid of becoming again interested in what I have learned from experience to be so transitory. I ardently hope I shall never all through life forget the truths which struck me so forcibly by Mamma's death-bed.[10]

Bishop O'Connor's response affirmed her insights but counseled moderation. Reading a novel now and then might be a good idea. His letter also contained his advice concerning her vocation:

And now, let me acquaint you with the conclusion I have reached in regard to your vocation. It is this, that you remain in the world, but make a vow of virginity for one year, to be renewed every year, with the permission of your director, till you or he thinks it well for you to omit or make it perpetual. This, I think, is what is best for you to do now, and as far as I can see, in the immediate future.[11]

Kate was frustrated by this counsel. If God willed her to live in the world, doing good with her position, money, and example, she would do it, though she was feeling deeply drawn to religious life.

On Sunday, November 18, Kate made her first vow of virginity before a painting of the Madonna in San Marcos. She took a card with a copy of the painting on one side and wrote the date on the back. Katharine kept this card throughout her life, tucking it into her missal during her later years. Her vow in San Marcos was a beginning, a first step toward fulfillment of a call that was becoming clearer in her own heart.

The European tour continued. How much of Kate's interior struggle her family knew is uncertain. But while they were enjoying the sights, she was finding everything lifeless like the dry bones Ezekiel saw piled high in the valley (see Ez 37:1-14). She wrote while staying at the Hotel Belle Vue, San Remo, on January 27, 1884:

Do please be patient with all the egos it will be necessary to use in opening my whole heart to you. It is a very sorrowful heart because like the little girl who wept when she found that her doll was stuffed with sawdust and her drum hollow, I, too, have made a horrifying discovery and my discovery like hers is true. I have ripped both the doll and the drum open and the fact lies *plainly* and *in all its* glaring reality before me: *All, all, all* (there is no exception) is passing away and will pass away. European travel brings vividly before the mind how cities have risen and fallen, and risen and fallen; and the same of empires and kingdoms and nations.... How long will the sun and moon, the stars continue to give forth light? Who can tell? Of one thing alone we are *sure*. In God's own time—then shall come the Son of Man in great power and majesty to render to each according to his works.

And now to return to the little girl. What was the consequence of her finding out that her doll was stuffed with sawdust? She says she does not wish to play with dolls anymore.... Now, dear Father, that is my case. I am disgusted with the world. God in his mercy has opened my eyes to the fact of the *vanitas vanitatis,* and as he has made me see the vile emptiness of this earth I look to him, the God of Love, in hope.[12]

Kate goes on to credit her mother's life of service to God as the major influence on her own life. Her mother saw the vanity of the world and chose not to be of it. Kate, in her way, would follow the holy woman's example.

The correspondence continued throughout the remainder of her travels. In it she listed the sacrifices she had been making, outlined her prayer schedule, and asked permission to receive the Eucharist four times a week.

The Drexels returned to the United States in May. In June, Kate wrote to Bishop O'Connor that she was not happy in the world: "There is a void in my heart which only God can fill."[13]

Last Trip With Her Father

Though her heart felt empty, Kate's life was full of activity. Not long after they returned from Europe, she and her father attended the installation of the new archbishop of Philadelphia, Patrick John Ryan. He later would become closely involved with Katharine and her spiritual journey.

In September of 1884, Mr. Drexel and two of his business associates traveled to the Pacific Northwest as the guests of the Northern

Pacific Railroad. They were going to see whether the railroad's bonds would be a good investment for their firm. Kate, Elizabeth, Louise, and their cousin, Mary Dixon, whose mother had recently died, went along.

The adventurous trip included a four-day visit to Yellowstone National Park—and an arrest on the charge of having removed some lava rock and other mineral specimens from their natural location. The offense was unknowingly committed since the Wyoming law had just been passed. All were acquitted at a trial held in a country store.

In Tacoma, Washington, the girls attended Mass at a small church and discovered its pastor was a priest the Drexels had once met in Rome. In addition to his small church, he also ministered to Native Americans in a number of missions. After seeing one of the missions, Kate promised to buy a statue for the chapel there.

Later she did just that, using $100 of her recently established $200-a-month allowance. She worried that her father might think her purchase extravagant, but in keeping with the Drexels' way of supporting one another, he was enthusiastic about her decision. The statue was the first of a lifetime of gifts that Katharine would give to Indian missions.

Having finished their business and sightseeing, the travelers returned home in early October.

The Death of Francis Drexel

The following February, 1885, a few days after visiting San Michel and after a long walk in Philadelphia with Louise, Francis caught a cold that developed into pleurisy. With a doctor's care and Elizabeth and Kate's devoted nursing, he began to recover. By February 12 he was well enough to play the organ.

Three days later he spent his morning in quiet meditation and reading. Kate, his nurse for the day, heard something and saw her father slumped back into his chair. She hurried to him but quickly saw he was dying and ran to St. Patrick's Church for a priest.

Meanwhile, one of the Drexels' servants took a cab to St. John's parish and brought back a priest. Neither clergyman arrived in time, and when Kate returned her father was dead. In just over two years, the girls had lost both parents.

Mr. Drexel's Pontifical Requiem Mass was celebrated by Archbishop Ryan at St. Mary's. Over two thousand people attended, spilling out of the packed church. Rich and poor, powerful and disenfranchised, famous and unknown, all came to pay tribute to the man who had touched their lives.

Francis Drexel had not wanted a eulogy at his funeral, but he was eulogized in newspapers across the land. The Philadelphia *Standard's* memorial described him this way:

Most unassuming and unostentatious in manner, he never tired of doing good; and never cared that the world should know of his benefactions. In his unbounded charity he most cordially cooperated with his wife and since her death which occurred about two years ago, with his daughters, who inherit from both sides not only great abundance of this world's good, but what is far better, the memory and example of good deeds that bring with them the choicest blessings.[14]

Mr. Drexel's estate was valued at $15.5 million. After some personal bequests, 10 percent was distributed to twenty-nine charities. These included the Cathedral of St. Peter and St. Paul, other churches and schools, orphanages, hospitals (including the only non-Catholic institution receiving a bequest, the German hospital, later called Lankenau Hospital after his brother-in-law), a widows' asylum, and religious orders.

The remaining 90 percent was put into a trust for his daughters. To safeguard them from fortune hunters, he stipulated that Elizabeth, Katharine, and Louise could spend only the trust's income as it was distributed annually by the trustees. He had made provision for children of his daughters as well as a plan for the estate if his daughters should die childless.

If one of his daughters should die without heirs, her share of the inheritance would be passed on to the surviving siblings. If the last daughter died without an heir, the trust would be dissolved, and the money distributed in the same proportion to the twenty-nine charities that had received the original tithe of 10 percent.

Mr. Drexel thus left a will that surprised the world and gave eloquent testimony to his generosity.

❧ FOUR ❧

Discerning Her Vocation

O nce again the long arm of extended family reached out to embrace the Drexel sisters. As she had done after Hannah Drexel's death, their Aunt Ellen Drexel provided a place for the girls to live. Uncles Anthony Drexel and John Lankenau looked after them with great love.

After a short while, the young women moved into San Michel and eventually into 1503 Walnut Street, keeping both family homes open. They continued the Dorcas outreach to needy families and imitated their parents' involvement with other charitable works.

Early Missionary Efforts

During this time, Elizabeth had an idea that would expand the efforts Mr. Drexel had begun in helping orphaned boys. Since these youngsters often left an asylum with no training for a life's work, she thought of building an industrial school for boys that would do just that. The school would be named St. Francis Industrial School, and it would be built on two hundred acres that Elizabeth purchased not far from San Michel.

Kate and Louise contributed time and ideas to the project as well. Such mutual support was a reality throughout their lives: the "All Three," as they called themselves, helping one another.

Soon yet another opportunity to help others found the Drexels; it literally came knocking on their door! Not long after Francis Drexel's death, two missionaries to Native Americans visited the Walnut Street home. Bishop Martin Marty, O.S.B., the vicar apostolic of Northern Minnesota, and Rev. Joseph Stephan, director of the Bureau of Catholic Indian Missions, spoke with Kate.

They explained the contract system that funneled federal money into the missions by way of a hundred-dollar stipend for each student enrolled in a religious school in Indian Territory. However, they added, no help was given in building or staffing the schools. That was up to the missionaries, and they needed money.

Kate was eager to help. Besides giving a generous contribution to St. Stephen's in Montana, and later, funds to build St. Catherine's in New Mexico, she would continue to support the missionaries' work for years to come. She and the missionaries forged a lasting friendship born of a common passion to evangelize and educate Native Americans.

But remaining in the world and quietly doing good works with her inheritance were not enough for Kate. Her desire to enter the religious life was growing stronger, and she continued to exchange letters with Bishop O'Connor. She wrote to him in August of 1885:

The question then, of my state in life resolves itself, it seems to me, into this one. What can I do for God's greater glory and service?... I presume He wishes me to be where I can first save my own soul, secondly, to do as much good as He intends with the means Dear Papa has left to me.... To tell the truth, it appears to me that God calls me to the religious life. But when is it prudent for me to obey the call? Next week? This Fall? This Winter? In what religious order?... You know I have a leaning to the contemplative life, but you and Father Ardia both say no to that; you know that I yearn to bring the Indians into Mother Church.[1]

Bishop O'Connor's objections were unchanged. He did not believe that her health would hold up to the rigors of convent life and thought that switching from her privileged existence to that of a religious would be too drastic a change. Kate could do more good in the world by her example than by being hidden away in a convent.

Obedient to her spiritual director, Kate continued using her inheritance to help those in need. In 1886 she purchased a building in Philadelphia to be used by the Sisters of Notre Dame as a "school for the colored." On June 17, the cornerstone was laid for St. Catherine's School in Santa Fe, New Mexico.

European Adventure

In the midst of these plans and new projects, Kate's health was deteriorating. Her father's death affected her deeply. Concerned, the three sisters planned another trip to Europe. They would stop at the mineral baths of Schwalbach for Kate, and wherever possible visit industrial schools, learning what they could to help with Elizabeth's project at home.

Anthony Drexel thought the trip was a wonderful idea and offered to take care of their finances while they were away. When the time came to leave, Johanna accompanied them as she had in the past. Martin, a valet, finished off the group. They sailed on July 31, 1886, landed in Liverpool on August 8, and wasted no time arriving at Schwalbach.

Doctors there recommended a five-week stay for Kate. She took mud baths and drank spring water twice a day while Elizabeth and Louise walked and walked and walked some more, sightseeing and touring the countryside and small villages.

The therapy seemed to work, and after finishing the program, Kate was ready to travel.

She kept a journal of their trip, which included visits to the Netherlands, Germany, Switzerland, Spain, Italy, and France. Her writings sparkled with enthusiasm for the places they visited. They also revealed a serious pilgrim. She was familiar with Scripture and scattered verses readily in her entries. She saw evidence of God everywhere she looked and was overwhelmed by God's love shown in the Incarnation.

> *Oct. 1st* ... Superb view of the Bernese Oberwald, in hazy, glorified distant light, high in cloudland, immediately below us a desolate stony valley. *Behold He cometh leaping from the mountains....* The condescension of the Incarnation never appeared to me more admirable. The contrast between the great CREATOR of the mighty forces of Nature and the Laws which restrain them and the *Verbum caro factum est* ["the Word was made flesh"].[2]

When an anticipated mountain view was shrouded in fog, she was reminded of God's presence, which sometimes cannot be perceived through human senses but is known only by faith: *"Indeed God is in this place and I knew it not."*[3] In keeping with her attraction to a contemplative order, her words recall the imagery in the mystical classic *The Cloud of Unknowing* as she waited in the prayer of quiet and then, in a fleeting moment of grace, experienced the Holy One:

> Clouds scudding through the narrow valley. It surrounded us. Desolation. Absolutely nothing to be seen. We wait ten minutes, still no view. Then for one minute the clouds are blown over the peaks, the sun shines on the white snow over their tops. Clouds

again spread around them, all is obscured. Again five minutes and again a peep at the sunlit mountain top. Simile of faith and hope.[4]

What she saw sometimes mirrored the struggle to follow her vocation:

A glacier [is] like an apostolic man. He is melted by God's love, the Sun which causes him to dash down the mountain side to fertilize the valleys. His novitiate is the passing through the wild, obscure mountain pass. Observed by none but God's love, the sun—and even this is often shut out from the torrent by the dreary mountain walls—the torrent dashes over the stones which oppose its downward course, directed by God's great Law of gravity.—It is opposed by the boulders, knocked by them into foam; but still it dashes on, on to the valley which it fertilizes, and into the thronged cities whose population receives its life from its broad, calm waters. This the will must be opposed, broken; but the man must follow out his sublime vocation.[5]

During her travels, Kate received a constant flow of letters from Fr. Stephan keeping her abreast of the situation with his Indian missions and the money she had given. She was also mindful of a promise she had made to Bishop O'Connor, trying unsuccessfully to find orders in Europe that would be willing to send priests to help in the Indian missions. Though she asked at some monasteries, she found no one.

The three sisters were eager to spend time in Spain, having been unable to convince their father to visit there on previous trips. They enjoyed two months in that country before moving on to Italy. In January they had the opportunity to attend Mass celebrated by the pope, and later to have an audience with him.

Remembering Bishop O'Connor's need for priests, Kate summoned her courage and mentioned the problem to Pope Leo XII:

> Kneeling at his feet, my girlish fancy thought that surely God's Vicar would not refuse me. So I pleaded missionary priests for Bishop O'Connor's Indians. To my astonishment His Holiness responded, "Why not, my child, yourself become a missionary?" In reply I said, "Because, Holy Father, sisters can be had for the missions, but no priests."[6]

After the audience, Kate felt sick all over. She hurried out of the Vatican and sobbed. She did not know what the pope had meant, but she was unsettled.

At times, we may have a deep-down knowledge that what has happened to us or has been said to us will have far-reaching ramifications, even if at the moment we do not know what those ramifications will be. Sometimes God uses another person's comment or some situation to reveal what is being asked of us. Such a moment can be overwhelming.

God's call can be frightening, taking us into places where we do not want to go, asking more than we think we can do. It need not be a call to religious life. It can be the call to marriage or to parenting a child with mental or physical challenges. We may feel inadequate in the face of a lost job or the lack of support from family or friends. Yet despite the anxiety, we recognize truth in the call.

Is that what happened to Kate when she heard Pope Leo's words? It is not important whether or not he was aware of his words' impact. God can use anything to stir a soul, especially one that so earnestly seeks him as Kate's did. Whatever her thoughts and reactions, whatever movement was stirring in her soul, the movement continued, hidden within, as she and her sisters moved on toward Paris.

One of Kate's letters shows three sisters in high spirits "smuggling" a St. Bernard puppy with them on the train. Since no pets were allowed in first-class accommodations, they wrapped it up like a baby, and Louise held it on her lap.

"Every time an R.R. official comes along," Kate reported, "at every stop of the train, we hide every bit of that babe under the afore-mentioned red shawl and read newspapers innocently over the bulky parcel, hoping to hide him, the babe."[7] The "babe" was then left with their Aunt Ellen, who was visiting Paris with her family. Martin left for home once the group arrived in Paris, finding a second puppy to bring back to San Michel, where it became a permanent fixture.

While in the famous city, the sisters dined with the Harje family, partners in their father's Paris firm. They attended morning Mass, had dresses made, and with an eye toward their own venture at home, visited a number of industrial schools run by the Christian Brothers.

In the midst of this bustle, Kate's most profound activity was taking place beyond the sight of others, in the interior of her soul. She longed to give herself more completely to God. Letters continued to pass between her and Bishop O'Connor.

In a letter dated March 5, 1887, he wrote to her that the work she was doing by supporting Indian missions with her inheritance was the work God wanted her to do:

You are making bountiful provision for the most abandoned and forlorn of God's creatures on this continent. You have the means, you have the brains, you have the freedom of action necessary to do this work well. In religion, you could direct your income to this or some other good purpose, but your talents and your energies would be directed by others.[8]

Across the ocean in Santa Fe, while Kate was nearing the end of her European tour, Archbishop Jean Baptiste Lamy dedicated St. Catherine's School, named in honor of Katharine's patron saint. Finally, on April 19, after a few weeks in England, Scotland, and Ireland, the Drexel sisters were sailing back to the United States. Once home, their lives again were busy with responding to numerous requests for aid.

Indian Missions and Other Charities

Fr. Stephan had repeatedly invited Kate, Elizabeth, and Louise to come west and see the destitution of Indian reservations for themselves. Not long after their return from Europe, the three sisters took him up on his offer. They left Philadelphia on September 19, 1887, and arrived in Omaha a few days later, where they met Bishop O'Connor.

Fr. Stephan met them at Norfolk Junction, and Kate, Fr. Stephan, and Bishop O'Connor continued in a wagon while Elizabeth and Louise rode ahead on horseback. Their traveling arrangements were a stark contrast to those of their recent tour of Europe. No first-class trains and hotels. No dressmakers and fine dining. This tour was taken instead over rough roads in buckboard wagons and on horseback.

They stopped first at Rosebud Agency in South Dakota, where they visited St. Francis Mission, built with Kate's money and named after her father's patron saint. Pine Ridge Agency was next. At Holy Rosary Mission, they met with Red Cloud, the famous Lakota[9] chief.

They presented the chief and his wife with gifts and were honored by an invitation to visit his home, which they did. Fr. Stephan informed Red Cloud that these women would help the mission and build a school for its children. Red Cloud never forgot, and he later came to their aid.

Bishop O'Connor returned to Omaha while the rest of the group traveled on to Stephan, South Dakota. There they visited Immaculate Conception Mission, also funded by Kate's donations. Then the party continued their journey through Indian Territory, visiting missions.

As they neared the Canadian border, the cold weather added further sufferings to the stark poverty and hardships they saw. The selfless service of the religious who labored in these missions made a lasting impression on Kate. After her return she funded schools for many Indian peoples who lived on land from Washington State to New Mexico.

Once these schools were built, she deeded them to the Catholic Indian Bureau, and Fr. Stephan obtained the federal government's contract of $100 per student. Between them, Fr. Stephan and Kate tried to find religious teachers to staff the schools. It was a difficult task.

Other demands made claims on Kate's time and attention. Her understanding of family members as "sacrament" for one another was evident in her decision early in 1888 to visit her ailing godfather, Uncle Joe Drexel. He had not been a practicing Catholic for some time, and "family intimacy, and relations with relations, is, I should think, a move in the right direction," Kate said.[10] As St. Francis of Assisi had admonished, she did not "preach" with words there but let her actions speak instead.

"You see, sisters mine, I am not doing any preaching," she wrote. "God & all the saints tell me what I am to do! I am getting to love & appreciate the family & their simple home life."[11]

Of course, there were also further requests for money. The newly formed Catholic University in Washington, D.C., asked for help from the Drexels, and they responded with $50,000, establishing the F.A. Drexel Chair of Moral Theology. St. Agnes Hospital received money to buy property.

Meanwhile, whatever else she was doing, Kate was involved in the internal struggle of discerning her vocation. On May 16, 1888, Bishop O'Connor penned another letter stating his conviction that Kate was where God wanted her to be:

> The more I reflect on the matter, the more I am persuaded that you are where God wishes you to be at the present.... The good work in which you are now engaged calls for all your time and your entire freedom and, as far as I can see, they give more glory to God, and do your neighbor more good, than anything you could accomplish in a religious community.[12]

Kate did not agree, but continued to do good in the world with her father's inheritance.

On July 28 of that year, Archbishop Ryan blessed the completed St. Francis Industrial School. Immediately two hundred boys from St. John's Orphan Asylum came to stay. Kate and Louise supported this project, but it became the focus of Elizabeth's charitable work.

Meanwhile, Fr. Stephan's call for help was persistent. Again, in September 1888, the Drexels traveled with him and Bishop O'Connor to see more Indian Territory of the Northwest. The conditions reflected the consequences of broken promises and degradation described in Helen Hunt Jackson's book *A Century of Dishonor,* which had deeply disturbed Kate. The Drexels returned home in early October, and though Kate and Bishop O'Connor were not traveling together through the Northwest, they were exchanging letters and opinions about her heightened desire to enter a religious order.

The Decision Is Made

When she was at home, life was as busy as ever. Katharine continued in her work but still anguished over the battle in her soul. She grappled with the increasing intensity of her call to give her life to God as a religious and her director's refusal to acknowledge it.

Many years later, in a conversation with Sr. Consuela Marie Duffy, Mother Katharine shared the agony she had experienced even as she took delight in Louise's decision to marry Colonel Edward (Ned) Morrell. Sr. Consuela wrote:

One day coming in from the summer house on the spacious Torresdale grounds where the two lovers had talked long together, Louise confided to Katharine that Ned and she both had the same idea, they both wanted to use their wealth to help those in need. Katharine knew then she would lose Louise, but she rejoiced at her sister's happiness in one worthy of her affection. She was glad, too, that her sister knew and could follow the vocation God had given her without the torment of soul she herself was experiencing.[13]

Not long after returning from the Northwest, Katharine reached her limit. She could no longer refuse the call she heard clearly from God. While she had obeyed Bishop O'Connor, and had followed his counsel, she had to be faithful to her relationship with the Lord. For years it had grown deeper and more intimate.

She wrote Bishop O'Connor, no longer to ask but finally to tell him what she knew: She was called to unite herself to God by living the vowed life of a religious.

After she wrote the letter, she let it sit for two weeks. How many people have poured out their souls onto paper, and then, afraid perhaps they had misstated something, or spoken too forcefully, or shared too much, have hesitated to send it? Once it is dropped into the mailbox, it cannot be recalled. Someone will read the words, and the world of the writer will be different from that moment on.

Kate must have felt that hesitation. Was she waiting to be sure of herself, or maybe to be confident that she had expressed the truth of her call strongly enough? Whatever made her wait, she finally sent the letter, dated November 26, 1888:

> May I trouble you to read the enclosed? It was written more than two weeks ago.... The sentiments in it remain the same, and have remained the same, only I am suffering greater anxiety lest Our Lord should deprive me of a life near Him in union with Him. My God! What can I desire better than this! "If thou *wilt* be perfect." I *will* it. Our Lord's words ring in my ears. How I wish to spend the rest of my life entirely given to Him by the three vows which would happily consecrate me to Jesus Christ! This night I feel a sadness out of which it is difficult to rally.
>
> It appears to me that Our Lord gives me the right to choose the better part, and I shall try to draw as near to His Heart as possible, that He may so fill me with His love, that all the pains I may endure in the religious life may be cheerfully endured for the love of Jesus, the Lord of Love. Do not, Reverend Father, I beseech you say, "What is to become of your work?" What is to become of it when I shall give it all to Our Lord? Will Our Lord at the day of Judgment condemn me for approaching as near Him as possible by following Him, and then leaving my yearly income to be distributed among the Missions, or for the Missions in some way that I *am sure* could be devised if only Our

Lord will free me from all responsibility save that of giving myself to Him? You allowed Louise to take Mr. Morrell. What about *her* income to the poor!

Are you afraid to give me to Jesus Christ? God knows how unworthy I am, and yet can He not supply my unworthiness *if* only He gives me a vocation to the religious life? Then joyfully I shall run to Him. I am afraid to receive your answer to this note. It appears to me, Reverend Father, that I am not obliged to *submit* my judgment to yours, as I have been doing for two years, for I feel so sad in doing it, because the world cannot give me peace, so restless because my heart is not rested in God. Will you, Reverend Father, please pardon the rudeness of this last remark, in view of this—that I am trying to tell you the truth?[14]

Katharine's soul would not be denied. Deferring to the divine truth he recognized in her passionate statement of vocation, Bishop O'Connor quickly affirmed her understanding of God's call in a letter dated November 30, 1888:

Yours of the 26th is received.

I had come to regard it as certain that Our Lord had chosen you for Himself, but, for reasons with which you are familiar, I inclined to think He wished you to love and serve Him as His spouse, but in society. This letter of yours, and your bearing under the long and severe tests to which I subjected you, as well as your entire restoration to health, and the many spiritual dangers that surround you, make me withdraw all opposition to your entering religion. In all that has passed between us in regard to your vocation, my only aim and anxiety have been to help you to discover God's will in the matter, and that, I think, is now sufficiently manifest. Something, too, which I heard, when in the East, a couple of weeks ago, of the well-meant *plans* made by those of your own flesh and blood to *entangle* you and Lizzie in mere worldly alliances, confirms me in this view of the case. A vocation like any other grace, *may* be lost, and they who have it should not be too much exposed, or expose themselves needlessly.

The only matter that, now, remains to be determined is, which order you should choose? Have you a decided preference for some one of them?[15]

Perhaps he only had been waiting for the conviction of her letter, the strength of claiming her call regardless of what anyone, particularly he, thought or said. Whatever the reason, Bishop O'Connor quickly switched his focus to finding a suitable order for Kate.

She had two main concerns. One she expressed in a letter of December 15: "I want a missionary order for Indians and Colored People."[16] The other requirement was the opportunity for frequent reception of the Eucharist.

Katharine's devotion to and need for the Blessed Sacrament had grown stronger through the years. Unlike today, frequent Communion was uncommon then. Katharine researched different orders to find ones that would permit it. The Benedictines and the Franciscans of Philadelphia were possibilities. She was attracted also by the Franciscans' missionary spirit.

On January 17, 1889, in the midst of Kate's planning, her sister, Louise, married Ned Morrell. Having been asked to celebrate the Mass, Bishop O'Connor allowed himself the pleasure of coming east for the occasion. Kate was one of four bridesmaids. Was she thinking of her own future vows as she walked down the cathedral's aisle?

Louise's marriage was the first change that disrupted the "All Three." Kate knew that her decision would be the next.

An Order of Her Own

Louise and Elizabeth supported Kate's decision, though Louise was quick to say that Kate should do nothing with her money until she had finished the novitiate and knew that she was going to stay. Kate was more concerned about Elizabeth. Louise was a married woman. Elizabeth would be alone.

While Louise and Ned were on their honeymoon, the sisters continued their practice of writing letters. Their love for one another shone through. Elizabeth told Louise that since her leaving, Kate had become her "very faithful companion."

> [She] has suddenly developed a love for all the things she hated but a short week ago—country going included. That very pleasing, small arch-deceiver has even gone so far as to forget all her aversion for horseback riding and declares that a short ride is the thing she positively pines for.[17]

The "All Three" would never again be together as they once had been, but always they would be part of one another's lives.

As Kate prepared herself to move into religious life and reviewed various orders, she also needed to devise a way to distribute her annual income. She shared her idea with Bishop O'Connor in a letter written February 12, 1889:

Would it not be well to organize a Bureau for Colored and Indian Missions? To lay aside a fixed salary for President, Vice President, and *all* members *necessary* for carrying on the work. Let these members live at Washington and let it be their *sole* and soul duty to attend to the affairs of the Bureau.[18]

Kate's idea included having bishops who would travel to missions and report to the bureau.

She drew her plan with broad strokes. Eager to enter the convent, she proposed leaving her income to her two sisters, who would then work out the details of the plan. Kate wanted to have everything settled so she could enter the novitiate on May 5, before the house at 1503 Walnut Street was closed and her sisters and brother-in-law left for a European tour.

While she was still deciding on an order, Bishop O'Connor had an inspiration. His idea, which came to him while at Mass, overwhelmed her. He wrote to her on February 16:

The more I have thought of your case the more convinced I become that God has called you to establish an order for the objects above mentioned. The need for it is patent to everybody. All the help the established orders can give, in the work, will be needed, but a strong order devoted to it exclusively is also needed. You have the means to make such an establishment. Your social position will draw to it subjects and friends without number. God has put in your heart a great love for the Indian and the Negroes. He had given you a taste and capacity for the sort of business which such a foundation would bring with it. All these things point more clearly, than an inspiration or a revelation could, to your duty in the premises.[19]

Kate did not share the bishop's enthusiasm. In her response she listed four reasons why she did not think she should found an order. The first was her deep desire for a contemplative life in which she could receive the Eucharist every day. Second, she did not believe she had the necessary virtue and charisma to be a foundress of a missionary order. Third, she thought that using established orders for her work would avoid the delays necessitated by red tape involved in establishing something new. Finally, Kate thought that the combined effort of many orders, funneled through the Catholic Indian Bureau, would be most efficient.

Bishop O'Connor was not convinced and, in his reply four days later, insisted that founding an order was God's will for her. He dismissed her objections as "scruples." Daily Communion could be made part of the rule. Some time for contemplation would keep her focused on her work. New orders are always raised up when a need is present.

Finally, addressing her concern that she lacked the virtues necessary, he wrote: "Even as a foundress you will have your faults, but God not you will do the work. He often makes use of very weak instruments. The question is not, will you be all that you should be, but does God will that you be His instrument."[20]

That wisdom is essential to remember no matter the vocation. What is lacking in every person will be made up by God's grace. Bishop O'Connor insisted that he was an instrument of the Church used to communicate this call to Kate.

He also tested the idea on a fellow bishop, Archbishop John Ireland of St. Paul, who responded enthusiastically: "Why, it is just the thing we needed. It is a great, an indispensable work. Miss Drexel is just the person to do it, and if she does not undertake it, it will remain undone."[21]

Kate desired to follow a life of poverty, and her inheritance was a constantly troubling issue. Joining a contemplative order and relinquishing her yearly income to the Bureau of Indian Affairs or some other central office was most attractive to her. That way she would be freed from concerns associated with so much money. In contrast, however, as a foundress she would be involved in all aspects of the order, including finances.

Sometime in March 1889, during a private retreat, Kate attended Mass and offered all she had been given back to God. She recorded these thoughts in her notes:

> Poverty of Spirit and not alone of spirit but actual abandonment, should He call, to all.... During Mass I gave back to the Eternal Father, that which God gave. I placed it in the hands of the spouse of Jesus, the Church, to hold or not to hold according to His Will. If we possess nothing, then we are not esteemed or praised. We can be humble.... I gave myself and all to Jesus, meek and humble of heart, to follow Him fearlessly. [22]

Finally, Kate's faith enabled her to accept the call to found a new order. She wrote to Bishop O'Connor on March 19, 1889: "The Feast of St. Joseph brought me the grace to give the remainder of my life to the Indians and colored, to enter fully and entirely into your views and those of rev'd Stephan as to what is best for the salvation of the souls of these people."[23]

She requested a letter of introduction from Bishop O'Connor to the superior of the Sisters of Mercy in Pittsburgh. Long familiar with that order, O'Connor thought its novitiate would be the best preparation for Kate. She and Lizzie visited in April, using their mother's maiden name, so none but a few knew who they were. After their visit, both sisters agreed that the convent on Webster Avenue would be a good place for Kate, and plans were made for her to enter on May 6.

✿ FIVE ✿

Years of Formation

In her decision to enter the religious life, Kate received the support of her family. Once again their deep affection wrapped around her when she needed it. Even though unable to understand or agree with her decision, they supported her because they loved her and wanted her happiness.

The Drexel family was rich with the love that does not hold too close, or smother, or attempt to change. How many young people leave home and family to follow the work of their heart without support, or worse, having to fight opposition? How many begin their adult life estranged from those they love, just when they need them the most? Kate truly was blessed.

> On the Annunciation I told Uncle Anthony ... of my intentions and future plans. Uncle Anthony dropped four or five tears; but he said he would not oppose anything which would contribute to my happiness. He thinks, however, that I am making the mistake of my life if I become a religious; yet he consents.[1]

Good-byes

So May 6, 1889, found Kate's brother-in-law, Colonel Morrell, with the three sisters saying good-bye to one another at a train station in Pittsburgh. The "All Three" realized that from that moment, their lives would never be the same. Kate was satisfying her heart's desire, which had grown more intense over the years. Her sisters let go of someone they longed to hold close. God's will be done.

Their parents had taught them well. A few weeks later Elizabeth wrote to a friend: "Let me assure you that on Kate's account we feel nothing but tranquility and contentment.... To say that we do not miss her and will not, is another matter."[2]

Newspapers spread the unbelievable story: An heiress of millions was entering a convent! The *Public Ledger* of Philadelphia wrote:

A sensation has been created by the announcement that Miss Kate Drexel, the 2nd daughter of the Late Francis A. Drexel, the distinguished banker, has decided to become a Nun.... While not tantamount to becoming a novice, this step on the part of the late celebrated banker's daughter will, without doubt, lead to her becoming one at the end of six months and finally to her permanently TAKING THE VEIL. Few who know the young lady doubt but that such will be the end of her first step taken yesterday in the renunciation of the world, with all that it contains of family, brilliant associations, and great wealth.... For the next six months she will undergo a probationary experience when, if she concludes to change her mind, it will be within her power to do so. If, at the expiration of that time, she still continues in her present frame of mind, then the strange spectacle will be presented of one of America's greatest heiresses laying aside all that so many thousands live for and adopting a new life as opposite as can be well imagined from that which she might be supposed to favor.[3]

Whatever the century, most people do not understand exchanging a life filled with privileges afforded by great wealth for one governed by vows of poverty, chastity, and obedience.

As the newspaper articles suggested, Katharine's decision to enter the convent made a stir. Days after becoming a postulant, she received a letter from Archbishop Ryan, telling her what good her example had already done.

Life as a Postulant

Katharine entered into her new life as a postulant with joy and enthusiasm. While the transition from an independent life of comfort and privilege to one of self-denial and obedience was difficult, it was also the life she longed for. Separation from her family was wrenching, but as she wrote to Bishop O'Connor, the prayers of so many had helped them through the moment, and the family connection was maintained.

Just as Kate and Lizzie had written to Louise and Ned when they had been on their honeymoon, once she had entered the convent Kate wrote to her family. She assured them: "Our Lord knows you & Lise & Brother Ned are part of myself, & when 'I' is in a prayer, I always mean the quartette. Please make the same contract with Our Lord for me, each of you."[4] The deep love and concern they had for one another, forged in childhood, remained; physically apart, they were united in spirit.

On May 8, her first day in the convent, Kate wrote to reassure them that she was not experiencing extreme hardships as they might have imagined:

My own darling sisters and brother,
I shall say about one word with regard to the good-bye of yesterday, and this you know already—God will bless you for it!—this thought rejoices me—And now, to what has occurred since I have been here. You are and shall always be I hope a part of my own self, and I a part of you, so you must know everything ... *Just as it is.*—

Well, on arriving at the convent Rev. Mother, and Mother Hilda, and Mother Josephine remained with me in the parlor for a half hour or so, and then I went up stairs to put on the postulant's gown. Now here is the real truth, so don't suspect me; the dress fits me sleeves and all, length of skirt—everything except that it is just a little too long waisted. I forgot to bring a tiny looking-glass with me and so I don't know how I look.... You would be pleased with my veil, which is of lace quite as fine and pretty as my Paris lace dress which Lise said she would have altered for herself. [5]

Katharine went on to tell her sisters and Ned details of the housekeeping, food, exercise, all the things she and her sisters would have shared. In another letter she detailed her daily routine, hour by hour, sure that it would help ease their minds.

Immediately, Katharine embraced life in the convent. She was quick to tackle menial tasks, such as cleaning up scraps left after sewing sessions. And the sisters found her a pleasure to have around.

Sr. Katharine had a keen sense of humor. She used to laugh most heartily at some of our absurdities. At recreation times when the novices were in the grove out at Saint Xavier Academy, she used to teach and lead us in Indian dances. At recreation she was delightful. [6]

Meanwhile, Katharine could at last weave evangelical poverty into the fabric of her life. She had already done so spiritually in her private retreat a couple of months earlier, but convent life offered the opportunity to live it out in a material way. This was evident to the other sisters shortly after she arrived. In a practice she maintained throughout her religious life, Katharine mended and darned everything from clothing to frayed napkins.

Though she adjusted happily to her new life and corresponded with family, she nevertheless suffered with the thought of founding a new order. Full of doubts about the endeavor and with tentative hope that perhaps founding a new order would not be necessary after all, she wrote to Bishop O'Connor on May 12:

This convent life is full of joy for me, and I am taking a most unmortified satisfaction in this respite from responsibility, which brings me peace. There is one thought, however, which causes me uneasiness. It is the thought of why I am here, viz., to prepare me for a future life of responsibility, and what is more, a life which is most apt to be one of opposition, trial, and subjection to criticism, even of the Church. Then, to have the very salvation of so many hang, as it were, upon my instrumentality! The undertaking you propose, Reverend Father, seems enormous, and I shall freely acknowledge that my heart goes down in sorrow when I think of it. To be the head of a new order! New orders always, I think, have to pass through the baptism of the cross! [7]

Of course, Bishop O'Connor immediately wrote back, informing Katharine that founding the new order was not up for consideration; it was already decided. He saw her doubts as a healthy sign that she was aware of difficulties ahead. He reminded her again that it was

God's work, not her own, and that God would see that she was up for the task.

So Katharine continued training as a postulant, with some exceptions being made to usual routines. She was given more than the usual amount of time to read and study to help prepare for becoming foundress of an order. She worked in the hospital and taught young children in school. On the financial front, she took care of administering the family money for missions and charities until her sisters returned from Europe.

Novitiate Years

In the autumn, Katharine received a letter from Bishop O'Connor that informed her of his failing health. Still, he expected to travel to Philadelphia to present her with the veil of a novice. Katharine rejoiced at that thought but was crestfallen when his health worsened and he was unable to attend her reception.

Archbishop Ryan presided at the ceremony on November 7, 1889, surrounded by three other bishops and many priests. Dressed in a satin bridal gown and bedecked with diamond rings and a diamond necklace, Katharine entered the chapel with eight young attendants leading the way. At one point during the ceremony, she left and returned garbed in the simple white habit of a novice.

The mixture of joy and sorrow in her life continued as Kate received news of her sister Elizabeth's engagement to Walter Smith, as well as news of Bishop O'Connor's continuing decline. Attempting to bring a smile to the bishop's face, Katharine sent him a humorous account of her attempts to keep order in a classroom of unruly elementary students.

Evidently, discipline was not her strength. Boys blowing whistles started a hullabaloo. At the signal, children began racing around the room, two boys started a fistfight, and someone started a fire in the fireplace. Kate's sternest look stopped the commotion for only a moment. Finally the sister from a room across the hall came to her rescue.

In the midst of life's challenges, Elizabeth's wedding was a bright spot for Katharine. In early January 1890, the Smiths left for a honeymoon trip that included traveling through Europe. Along with letters from her sister, Katharine continued to receive letters from Fr. Stephan about the Indian missions.

The news was not good. The school in St. Stephen, Montana, was without teachers, and the contract system was soon to be terminated by the new Commissioner of Indian Affairs.

News of family and friends made Katharine's emotions soar and plummet and rise again. Bishop O'Connor did not improve, and his doctor eventually sent him south to a warmer climate. At the end of January, Mother Sebastian and Sr. Katharine traveled to Florida to see whether they might bring Bishop O'Connor back to Philadelphia.

After two weeks, they did return with him, and Sr. Katharine was assigned to watch over him at Mercy Hospital in Pittsburgh. While caring for the bishop, Katharine learned that her sister, Elizabeth, had become seriously ill. Later, Elizabeth seemed to recover and had a nurse accompany her as she and her husband continued their travels. Happier news came later: Elizabeth was pregnant.

By mid-April, sensing his approaching death, Bishop O'Connor requested that he be returned to his own diocese in Omaha. On May 27 he died, and Katharine was devastated. How could she continue on her path without the spiritual guide who had helped map it out, and who had been her constant support?

When Archbishop Ryan came to visit on his way home from the

funeral, she told him as much. "If I share the burden with you, if I help you, can you go on?" he asked.[8]

His words sunk deep into her grateful heart like rain soaking parched ground, renewing her hope and courage. Her relationship with Archbishop Ryan moved to a new level. From that point on, as indicated by the closing of his letters to her, *"Your father in God,"* he became her intimate friend and trusted spiritual advisor.

Katharine continued to learn as much as she could about religious life while deepening her own spirituality. Some postulants were entering the Sisters of Mercy convent with the intent of joining Katharine's new order. She and Archbishop Ryan were involved in deciding on a location for the new motherhouse. After considering a number of possibilities, they decided on a sixty-acre site nineteen miles from Philadelphia in what is now called Cornwells Heights. The motherhouse was to be built in the style of the Spanish missions in the Southwest.

On September 26, 1890, death again tore at Katharine's heart. Elizabeth's precarious health had taken a serious turn. Katharine hurried to see her at San Michel, now the Smiths' home, but by the time she arrived the child her sister had so eagerly awaited had been stillborn, and Elizabeth herself was dead.

How many memories must have filled Katharine's heart as she knelt before the coffin that held her sister with her tiny baby in her arms. The hallways and rooms that once held their childhood laughter, secrets, and celebrations now held the family's grief.

Another tragedy hit at the end of the year as Katharine was preparing to make her final vows. After continual mistreatment by the U.S. government and a year of drought that brought them to near-starvation, some Lakota Indians vented their anger in a violent revolt on the Pine Ridge Reservation. A number of buildings were burned, some of them close to the Holy Rosary Mission.

While on retreat, Katharine prayed for protection for those who lived and worked at Holy Rosary. Only the intercession of Red Cloud prevented its destruction by angry young braves. The uprising came to a tragic end when American cavalry slaughtered over two hundred Lakota men, women, and children in what became known as the Wounded Knee Massacre.

A New Order

At last the day of Katharine's first profession arrived. She was ready to leave the novitiate and begin her new order. The troubling issue of what to do with her inheritance had been put to rest. Archbishop Ryan asked only that Katharine promise that if he deemed it necessary, she would renounce her income and the control of it. But for the present she remained administrator of her funds.

A design for the order's habit at last had been chosen, incorporating the Benedictine scapular. Later that year, after permission had been obtained from Rome, the Franciscan rope cincture was added. A member of the Third Order Franciscans, Katharine had deep devotion to St. Francis and shared his love of "Lady Poverty."

On February 12, 1891, Katharine made her first profession and received the black veil from the hands of Archbishop Ryan. To the vows of poverty, chastity, and obedience she added another: "To be the mother and servant of the Indian and Negro races according to the rule of the Sisters of the Blessed Sacrament; and not to undertake any work which would lead to the neglect or abandonment of the Indian and colored races."[9] After receiving her vows, Archbishop Ryan appointed her superior of the new order, the Sisters of the Blessed Sacrament. He added "for the Indians and Colored Races" to its official name.

The sisters thought they would have their first opportunity to serve the Indians when they learned that St. Stephen's School in Montana had closed for lack of sisters to staff it. Mother Katharine and Sr. Patrick visited the school with an eye toward readying it for a new academic year to be directed, she thought, by her own sisters.

Archbishop Ryan was wiser, however, and did not give permission. He knew that the eager young missionaries, with only one professed sister among them, needed time to grow spiritually—not only individually, but also as a community, grounding itself in the wisdom and ways of religious life. But where would they do that?

The motherhouse, named St. Elizabeth's in honor of the patron saint of Katharine's sister, was far from ready. So Mother Katharine and Sr. Inez, who was loaned from the Sisters of Mercy convent to be temporary novice mistress, moved into San Michel on July 1. Once home to the Drexel family, it now opened its arms to Katharine's spiritual family. The house and grounds provided a place of warmth and nurture for the new order. Ten novices and a postulant arrived soon after.

Almost immediately after she arrived at San Michel, Mother Katharine received her first visitor, Archbishop Francis Janssens from the financially troubled diocese of New Orleans. He requested help and received it from that date until his death. He and Mother Katharine become correspondents and lifelong friends, both concerned with spreading the Catholic faith and opening doors of opportunity for blacks through education.

Not everyone was enthusiastic about making reparation to members of the oppressed races. The laying of the cornerstone of the new motherhouse on July 16 drew threats from some surrounding farmers who were not happy to have as neighbors an order vowed to serve Native Americans and blacks. Dynamite had been found near the site.

Unaware of the danger, the sisters dressed in their new habit for the first time and gathered for the ceremony. Archbishop Ryan, Colonel Morrell, and the architect had arranged to have plainclothes police guard the area. Violence was averted, but the threat was an indication of the resistance and prejudice to be encountered in the future.

Growing Into a Community

Members of the new order were anxious to be sent into mission territory. Though disappointed by Archbishop Ryan's refusal to allow them to go to St. Stephen's, they would not have long to wait. Meanwhile, formation into a community of spiritually strong women was their primary task. The motherhouse was still under construction and lacked electricity, running water, and heat. Nevertheless, on December 3, 1892, led by Mother Katharine and with true pioneer spirit, the sisters moved in.

Though she doubted her fitness to shepherd such an order, Katharine was well prepared. Nothing but deep faith and love for God could prepare her to embrace such a drastic change of lifestyle and the burdens of being a foundress, but such faith and love were hers. A contemplative, she found strength and courage in prayer and the sacraments, especially the Eucharist.

Her life experiences prepared her for other demands. She was well educated, not only through academic studies but also by life in a large household. As a girl and young woman, Katharine had been responsible for overseeing the household at San Michel. Having helped her mother in the charitable works of Dorcas, perhaps she had learned the importance of keeping careful records as much from her mother as from her banker father.

Because of her family background, Katharine was socially flexible. She had seen firsthand the poverty and need of Native Americans, who had welcomed her into their homes. She had conversed easily with the poor of Philadelphia who came to the family's back door. Yet she had moved as well among ambassadors and popes.

Finally, Katharine had experience in dispersing large sums of money from her inheritance and had funded a number of missions before entering the convent. From her parents she had learned that wealth and good fortune were God's gifts given to them for the welfare of others. Francis and Emma Drexel were good stewards, and their daughters had learned from their example.

Katharine knew from the first mention of founding an order that a large amount of her time and energy would be spent negotiating the bureaucratic as well as theological labyrinths encountered when establishing something new in the Church. She would spend years writing and rewriting the Rule and Constitutions for her order. As a religious, Katharine could completely give herself as well as her fortune to serve God in Native Americans and blacks, but over her lifetime that service took many forms.

While she was overseeing construction and operations of missions across the country, she was also mother general and novice mistress at home. She administered the income from her inheritance and later from the combined amounts of her sisters' inheritance as well, reviewing requests for help that continually came to her and to the Sisters of the Blessed Sacrament. Often she would go herself to see the need before deciding what course of action would be most helpful, spending up to six months a year traveling.

She corresponded with Fr. Stephan, who kept her abreast of developments and needs that he saw in the Indian Territory. She had already begun work in the South by funding some of Archbishop Janssens' apostolates, and she would continue to expand the order's efforts in that part of the country.

Katharine was blessed with the ability to juggle many projects at once, and it is a good thing she was. She spent much of her adult life doing just that. Whatever her work, it enabled many others to fulfill their call to missionary life.

In the beginning, however, her place was with her sisters. Even though they were not traveling to far-off places, the sisters had begun missionary work at home. When they moved into their new mother-house, they brought with them students, black and white, who had been housed and taught together in one of the cottages at San Michel. That act alone was blazing new ground.

Early in 1893, Providence School was opened on the grounds of the motherhouse. Despite that work, the women dreamed of being sent further afield. Little more than a year later the long-awaited day arrived. Sisters of the Blessed Sacrament were sent out as missionaries.

❧ SIX ❧

Missions and the Rule

Along with Sr. M. Evangelist, Mother Katharine traveled to assess the needs of St. Catherine's school in Santa Fe. Funded by her before her entrance into religious life, it had been run by a series of different orders but was closed when no more teachers could be found.

Archbishop Ryan gave permission for the Sisters of the Blessed Sacrament to take over the school. The delighted order sent out nine missionaries. The first group of four left on June 13, 1894. The second group followed a week later. The tearful but joyous farewells were just the first of many to come.

In the few days between missionary departures, Mother Katharine traveled to Virginia looking for property on which to build a school for black girls, a complement to Louise's industrial school for boys. She chose some land adjacent to her sister's and purchased six hundred acres in Rock Castle. This was only one of many times throughout her active life when she would be physically shuttling between projects.

No stranger to railway stations during these travels, Katharine had many tales to tell. In one letter she described how she rushed to catch a train in St. Louis after the connecting train had arrived in the station an hour and twenty minutes late:

Two minutes to catch train! It was a picture, not indeed of religious gravity, to behold first a porter with a telescope in each hand; secondly, M.M. Katharine in her *fastest* walk—you all know that is rather speedy—thirdly, Sr. Josephine about five feet behind, her limbs unused very properly to the double quick footsteps of her mother; fourthly, in the rear, speeding as quickly as her frame permitted, Sr. Louis Bertrand. Soon the walk became a genuine run, as the porter looked back and said, "Ladies, we'll have to go quick, one minute to reach the train." So up the long depot we ran, through labyrinths of people as we neared the gate; but regardless of all but one thought—the train—we wound around now one group of travelers, now another, making a way for ourselves—1st, the porter; 5 ft. behind M.M.K.; 5 ft. behind her, Sr. Josephine; 5 ft. behind her, Sr. Louis B.!! [1]

Modern travelers can identify with the result: After boarding the train on time, Katharine, her companions, and the other passengers waited for over an hour before it departed.

Nevertheless, Katharine, who had crossed the West on buckboards and horseback, was not daunted by inconvenience. An adventuresome spirit, she eagerly tried any mode of transport that would deliver her to the missions.

Growth of the Early Missions

Katharine not only had a vision for establishing and supporting missions across the country. She also became personally involved in their evolution from idea to reality. When Bishop O'Connor had first suggested she found an order, Katharine had known that in doing so she would embrace the cross of being physically busy with administrative duties.

Nevertheless, she willingly relinquished her personal desire for contemplative life and also her desire to serve as a missionary. Instead, she gave her talents to creating opportunities for others. Her gaze was never on herself or what she wanted, but it was on her Lord and the will of God.

During May of 1895 Mother Katharine made yet another trip to St. Catherine's, bringing two more sisters to augment the community. The mission received another visitor that year. The apostolic delegate to the United States, Cardinal Francesco Satolli, came with Archbishop Placide-Louis Chapelle of Santa Fe, after his installation, marking the cardinal's first encounter with Sisters of the Blessed Sacrament.

Closer to home two months later the cornerstone was laid for St. Francis de Sales School in Rock Castle. Mother M. Mercedes once told an interesting story of their arrival for the ceremony. She and Mother Katharine had been delayed and had taken a later train to Richmond than intended. It pulled in under a dark night sky.

Mother Katharine was willing to remain at the station and wait for morning Mass and a chance to buy breakfast before traveling on to Rock Castle, but the station closed after their train arrived. Forced to stand outside, trying to decide what to do, they were met by an older black gentleman with a horse-drawn carriage. He told them they were expected to spend the night at the Franciscan convent of St. Joseph in town.

Surprised but appreciative, the two sisters climbed into his carriage. Once at the convent, he carried their bags to the door and left. They rang many times before rousing anyone.

As it turned out, no one had been expecting them, nor had the Franciscans sent the older gentleman to meet the travelers at the station. Mother Katharine commented that he must have been St. Joseph, who did not want them out alone so late at night.

The sisters found 1896 to be another busy year. Cardinal Satolli visited Philadelphia and the motherhouse before returning to Santa Fe at Archbishop Chapelle's request. Once there he again visited St. Catherine's. Having been impressed by the order and their work, he promised to mention them to Pope Leo XIII when he returned to Rome.

Also during this year Fr. Stephan helped Mother Katharine purchase land in Arizona for a mission to the Navajos. Together they spent much time looking for an order of priests to work there. Finally, in 1897 the Franciscans of the Cincinnati Province accepted the call.

Some other encouraging news had reached Mother Katharine on February 16 of that year. Rome sent a "Decree on the Community," the Vatican's first step in sanctioning the new community. Perhaps Cardinal Satolli's good words had made a difference.

Archbishop Ryan instructed Mother Katharine to have the order's Rule translated into Latin and sent to Rome, which she did. However, the response instructed Mother Katharine to conform the Rule to recently compiled directions for religious orders, the *Normae*. Work on the Rule seemed never-ending, but it was woven in and out of the order's engagement with missions.

During the following years, activity in the West and in Virginia demanded attention. Two Franciscan priests and one brother went to Arizona in October 1898 and moved into a renovated trading post. Financed by Mother Katharine, the move was the beginning of St. Michael's Mission.

Over the next four years she would be involved in procuring land and building a school there. The Franciscans, who faithfully lived out their vow of poverty relying on Divine Providence, were an inspiration to the foundress. Their efforts to learn and speak the Navajo language won them many friends among native people who felt comfortable visiting their home.

Eventually their labor resulted in a Navajo dictionary and catechism. Meanwhile, Mother Katharine had plans for St. Michael's Boarding School drawn up by an architect in Philadelphia. She enlisted the Franciscans' help in finding a contractor.

A woman who concerned herself with details as well as with the larger vision, Katharine paid careful attention to all aspects of construction. Her letters were full of references to water access, possible flooding, rebates on the cost of shipping, and even how to prevent mice from destroying goods stored in empty buildings. The amount of information and number of projects that filled her mind at any one time was staggering. She was a contemplative, a missionary, yes, but also an astute businesswoman.

While plans for St. Michael's continued, work on St. Francis de Sales School was completed. When Mother Katharine and Mother M. Mercedes arrived there on July 17, 1899, to prepare for the other sisters and students who would soon fill the buildings, they were surprised by news of a suspicious fire. Just as someone had been unwilling to have their order's motherhouse nearby, it seemed that someone else did not want to have a boarding school for black girls in Rock Castle. Luckily, the fire damaged only the barn and did not delay either the coming of nine other sisters a week later or the opening of school in October.

True to their vision of missionary work, the Sisters of the Blessed Sacrament at St. Francis de Sales did not limit their work to teaching school. They made home visits and visited prisoners as well, eventually starting a library for the inmates.

When not afield, Katharine was at the motherhouse continuing to refine the Rule. Archbishop Ryan had given her more help, appointing Fr. Herman J. Heuser, a theology professor, to make sure each detail complied with canon law.

A Firsthand Look

In 1902 Katharine made two trips to Arizona. The second was in late summer, and Josephine Drexel, her niece, accompanied her for part of the trip. After checking on progress at St. Michael's, Josephine and Katharine traveled through the Indian Territory, seeing firsthand how missions she had funded were operating.

Mother Katharine was disappointed to find few full-blooded Indians in the schools. The government's offer of land to anyone with Indian blood had attracted many mostly white people to the area. Her frustration showed in a letter written to her sisters after the trip: "I am still dazed at the discovery made in one trip to the Indians, where in their own land, their own specially reserved territory, so few Indians, comparatively, are to be seen. White people and white people always, and white Indians, except in the unbeaten paths."[2]

She envisioned a world where races intermarried and eventually no one would be able to tell one race from another. But in the present time, she did not want Native Americans to be cheated out of land or opportunity because they lacked education that would enable them to compete and confront those who would take advantage of them. For this reason as well as for evangelization, she built and funded numerous schools.

White people's dominating presence in the mission schools was only one problem to be overcome at St. Michael's. Another was the Navajos' understandable reluctance to send their children to a boarding school. Although Mother Katharine and the Franciscans had talked with parents two years earlier, by the time St. Michael's School was ready to open in 1902, the parents had to be convinced again to leave their children in the sisters' care.

Nevertheless, by December 3, the first day of school, forty-seven students were enrolled. Many parents stayed nearby for a few weeks, sleeping outside and watching the sisters during the day. They must have been pleased with what they observed: The following year, enrollment doubled, and it eventually reached 150. Mother Katharine's goal was to evangelize the children and equip them with skills needed to enter into mainstream American life with dignity and possibilities for success.

Whether she was at home or visiting missions, the foundress often had the Rule in her thoughts. By 1903 it was ready to be scrutinized by the community. The superiors of every convent read it to their sisters. A space was provided for each sister to sign the document if she agreed with the contents.

In 1904 Katharine made some changes, and the amended Rule was again read to all sisters for their approval. After being checked against canon law and translated into Latin, the Rule was sent to the apostolic delegate, Cardinal Diomede Falconio. Not satisfied, he wanted detailed financial information about the order and its funding of missions and other works. On December 10, after the requested material was gathered, the Rule was sent to Rome.

To the South

The year 1904 was also a time of visiting the South. Mother Katharine had funded many missions there and wanted to know how they were functioning. She kept detailed notes of her travels and observations, documenting conditions of black Catholics in the South.

Just as the lack of Native Americans in the western mission schools disappointed her, Katharine was surprised by the lack of black Catholics in the churches. While individual mission churches that had received funding from her had complied with her stipulation to reserve an aisle of pews from front to back for blacks, few people of color filled the seats. In some instances it seemed churches had taken her money with no intention of evangelizing blacks or encouraging them to attend Mass there. In other churches, blacks were made to feel unwanted by practices such as the insistence that they receive Communion after whites, or that they attend separate missions.

Stories of mistreatment of blacks in some southern Catholic churches had reached Rome and elicited a response from Cardinal Girolama Giotti. In April of 1904, American archbishops decided to send out copies of the cardinal's letter instructing bishops across the country to take action to remedy the situation. Not much changed.

In 1905 an organization was begun that had been suggested by Archbishop Ryan with Katharine's support: The Catholic Board for Mission Work Among the Colored People. Cardinal Giotti was made its head. The need was great but workers were few. So the Sisters of the Blessed Sacrament would soon be heading to the South.

In June 1904, Bishop Thomas Byrne of Nashville asked the foundress if her sisters could operate a school in his diocese. Katharine offered money but did not immediately send sisters. It would take a chance meeting with Bishop Byrne while both were in the West, and a later conversation at St. Michael's mission, to change her mind.

The bishop had seen a property that would be perfect for an industrial school. The order was willing but had to make sure he realized that they would not, as he wished, make the school available to Catholics only. Such a policy was not acceptable to these missionaries.

The many challenges offered by the South became apparent when the house came up for sale the following year. Mother Katharine and Mother M. Mercedes viewed the property from inside a carriage. The owner would never sell to someone who would open a school for blacks.

A lawyer made the purchase for her on February 2, keeping his client's identity a secret. Once details of the transaction were published, the former owner tried to buy back the house. A long, drawnout battle was waged on many fronts, including in the newspaper.

Katharine was surprised to see a personal letter she had written to the former owner published for all to read. Neighbors approached her, asking her to reconsider. "There are a number of localities in and around the city where Colored People live," they insisted, "and where no objection would be made to the location of your school."[3]

Mother Katharine did not budge. She believed that those who had been deprived of so much for so long deserved only the best, and that certainly did not mean property that no one else wanted. The school, Immaculate Mother Academy and Industrial School, opened on September 5, 1905. Over one hundred students had enrolled by the end of its first year, and an additional school building was erected in 1907.

The missionary work of the Sisters of the Blessed Sacrament was two-pronged: to evangelize and to educate. The first priority was to spread knowledge and faith in God, bringing membership in the Church to as many as possible. The second was to do humanitarian work by providing education, means of self-support, and help in whatever ways they could to bring dignity and fullness into the lives of those they served.

Approval of the Rule

While dealing with the establishment of this new school, Mother Katharine was also renewing her efforts on the Rule. Msgr. Thomas Kennedy, a rector of the American College in Rome, had visited in

January 1905 and informed the foundress that some points needed more work. After continual effort, she made a twelve-day retreat in March 1906 to discern God's will in the matter. Then, with the help of Fr. Heuser, who checked the document for conformity to canon law, the Rule was again ready for Rome.

A surprise visit from Mother Frances Cabrini helped Katharine decide how it would be sent. Sitting with her in a parlor at the mother-house, Katharine graciously accepted Mother Cabrini's thanks for hospitality the Sisters of the Blessed Sacrament had shown two of her own sisters while they were in the area. Then, knowing that Mother Cabrini had written a Rule for her order, Mother Katharine asked for advice.

What if her Rule became bogged down in Rome once it arrived there? Mother Cabrini offered this counsel: "If you want to get your Rule approved, you go yourself to Rome and take it with you."[4]

Mother Cabrini's suggestion seemed impossible to Mother Katharine, considering her duties as novice mistress. However, Archbishop Ryan gave enthusiastic permission, and by May 11, 1907, the foundress and Mother M. James were sailing to Rome.

Once there, Katharine was surprised that Msgr. Kennedy did not share her sense of urgency. The Rule was foremost in her mind, but other concerns filled his. Besides, the priest he had chosen to translate had died, and he had no candidates for a replacement. Katharine prayed to her patron saint, St. Catherine of Sienna, for assistance in finding some "holy men" to help her cause.

In just two days, Mother Katharine again heard from Msgr. Kennedy. At a dinner he had met Fr. Joseph M. Schwartz, C.SS.R., who revealed in conversation that he had just finished helping the Franciscans of Philadelphia finish their Constitutions. A little talk revealed that Fr. Schwartz was from Philadelphia and knew of Katharine's father and his generous bequest. He had agreed to help the young order himself. He also recommended someone to translate the Rule into Latin.

Work progressed quickly by Roman standards, and Mother Katharine took time to enjoy the spiritual offerings of the city. She visited shrines and churches, attended Masses, and spent time in adoration of the Blessed Sacrament. She made time for a little sightseeing, and she and Mother M. James had an audience with Pope Pius X. By July 5, Cardinal Satolli informed them that the Sacred Congregation would consider their Rule the following day.

The Rule was approved, and the pope gave his required endorsement as well. As is the common practice, the "Decree of Definitive Approbation of the Congregation and Experimental of the Constitutions" was given for five years. After that time, if the Rule proved itself in lived experience, it would be permanently granted.

On July 18 the sisters began their return voyage. They arrived in New York on August 3 and proceeded to the motherhouse, where overjoyed sisters welcomed them home.

On November 23, in accordance with the Rule, the first general chapter was convened. Mother M. Katharine was elected the first superior general. Sr. M. Juliana assumed the role of novice mistress that had been held by the foundress since Mother Inez had returned to the Sisters of Mercy in 1891. The Sisters of the Blessed Sacrament for Indians and Colored People was an official order of the Catholic Church.

More Missions and Final Approval of the Rule

Mother Katharine and the Sisters of the Blessed Sacrament continued their missionary work. A number of sisters were teaching catechism in the government Indian school in Carlisle, Pennsylvania, as well as running a school for black children.

While visiting there in January 1911, Mother Katharine learned that Archbishop Ryan was seriously ill. He had last visited the motherhouse two months earlier and had asked for prayers since he was nearing eighty. Still, the call about his deteriorating condition was a surprise.

Katharine immediately returned to Philadelphia to be with him at the hospital. She drew strength from his graceful approach to death. Visiting him almost every day, she reassured the archbishop of his importance in making the order a reality.

"You are the Foundress, and *I am the founder with you*," he said.[5] "You are the founder. If it had not been for your interest, I could not have gone on," Katharine told him on her last visit.[6]

Archbishop Ryan died on February 11. Mother Katharine was overcome with grief. He had helped guide her through the order's early years of formation and into its present state.

The archbishop had become her dearest friend, confidant, and spiritual director. His death left an empty place that no other could fill. Her cheeks constantly stained with tears, she stayed at her order's convent of Our Lady of the Blessed Sacrament until after the funeral, and then plunged again into the swirling demands of her work.

The following years were filled with new missions and with the final approval of the Rule. The year 1912 began with a trip to Ohio, where Bishop Hartley had requested help in opening a school in Columbus. In the spring Mother Katharine traveled to visit missions in the West.

Next, with Mother M. Ignatius she went to New York, where they looked for houses to turn into a convent and school in Harlem. The two buildings they finally found were filthy and full of refuse.

Undaunted, Mother Katharine worked along with the other sisters making the houses ready.

She returned to Columbus, Ohio, to prepare that house and then moved on to Chicago, where once again she joined with other sisters cleaning and fixing up an old, dirty house that would become St. Monica's Convent. In the midst of this missionary fervor, Msgr. Kennedy informed Mother Katharine that she should be prepared to bring the Rule to Rome in November for final approval. Despite urging from the sisters to slow down and prepare herself physically for the trip, Katharine continued with a grueling schedule of travel and work overseeing missions.

In September she left to visit St. Catherine's in Santa Fe, with a stop scheduled in Cincinnati. Once in Santa Fe, her constant work and travel caught up with her. She became sick with typhoid and pneumonia, coming close to a nervous breakdown.

Mother Katharine was taken to the Albuquerque Sanitarium, and though her sisters were eager to go to her, she did not want them to make the trip. Her brother-in-law, Colonel Morrell, went instead. Once in Santa Fe he arranged to have Mother Katharine returned to the motherhouse with the best doctors to look after her. Katharine needed complete rest to recover, and the trip to Rome was postponed until the following April.

Requests for help continued to come from those laboring in missionary fields, and 1913 was as full as the previous year had been. Plans for building in New York were firmed up, and a school and church were built in Atlanta in honor of Archbishop Ryan. The Sisters of the Blessed Sacrament were invited to Boston, where they opened centers for catechesis and home visitations. The general council of the order also went over their Rule again in preparation for its final review.

By spring, Mother Katharine was well enough to travel. She and

Mother M. Mercedes sailed for Rome from New York on April 5. The two spent most of their time in the city polishing the Rule.

All their persistence and attention to detail paid off. On May 15 the final approbation was given. At long last, work on the Rule was finished.

After visiting Assisi, Florence, and Milan, Mother Katharine and Mother M. Mercedes traveled through other parts of Europe and Ireland on their way home, hoping to find some young women to join with them in serving black and Native Americans. They were successful in planting seeds that yielded vocations in later years. Sisters of the Blessed Sacrament revisited Ireland numerous times, and many young women crossed the ocean to join the order.

On June 29, the two sisters returned from their travels and once again were welcomed home by a joyous congregation now permanently established in the Church.

SEVEN

The Work Continues

As with her missions to Native Americans, Mother Katharine saw a solid moral education as the means to enable blacks to enter the mainstream of American life. The missions in New York, Chicago, and the Midwest were already addressing that need. While the education provided was Catholic, being Catholic was never a requirement for students in these mission schools.

Katharine also believed that if black students had the aptitude and desire for higher education, they should have the opportunity to pursue it. That put her in opposition to some who were in favor of eliminating high schools for blacks, wanting to provide vocational training instead. Despite such resistance, in 1915 Mother Katharine made opportunity for higher education a reality for black Catholic students in New Orleans.

Xavier University

Southern University was a college for black students in New Orleans. But residents near the college campus, uncomfortable with a black school in their midst, petitioned to have it relocated from their predominantly white neighborhood. In time, they were successful: The college was moved to Baton Rouge.

Nevertheless, the neighbors' relief was short-lived. The vacant buildings seemed like an opportunity to Fr. Pierre Lebeau, a Josephite priest who had long been concerned about the absence of a Catholic college for black students in the area. Mother Katharine was contacted.

In the past she had refused opportunities to come to New Orleans, unwilling to infringe on the work of the Sisters of the Holy Family, an order of black women who had a motherhouse there. However, since running an institution of higher learning was not a project that particular order would undertake, Mother Katharine enthusiastically embraced the idea.

She and Mother Mercedes traveled to New Orleans in early April to inspect the property quietly and found it suited their purpose well. Mother Katharine's reputation preceded her, and she knew better than to try to purchase the building herself. Instead a local man, recommended by the archbishop of New Orleans, bought it for her at a public auction. White residents of the area were angry when they realized that a school for black students would again fill the old Southern University buildings.

After overseeing renovations, Mother Katharine stretched social boundaries by assembling an integrated faculty. A course of study was developed, and Xavier University opened its doors in September 1915. Soon, white sisters studying beside black students would challenge Louisiana's segregation laws. The Sisters of the Blessed Sacrament were again ahead of their time.

In the beginning, day classes were offered for students in grades seven through eleven, as well as evening classes in sewing and typing, and some advanced level classes for qualified students. The following year twelfth grade was added, and the year after that, a two-year "normal school." Higher education for black Catholics had arrived in New Orleans.

Fr. Girault and Rural Louisiana Missions

However, higher education was only one end of the educational process that needed attention. Fr. Jean Marie Girault de la Corgnais had made Mother Katharine aware of the woeful condition of elementary schools for black children in rural Louisiana. This saintly French nobleman-turned-missionary had come to the United States to serve along the backwaters of rural Louisiana. He seemed Katharine's equal in the intensity and completeness with which he gave himself to God's work among the poor and forgotten.

Like Katharine, Fr. Girault was well educated and a man of many talents. With a little medical training, he was the only doctor many people there knew. He served at one time or another as, among other things, mayor, sheriff, coroner, school principal, architect, and lawyer. He won the admiration of local trappers and hunters, perhaps the most difficult of all his honors to obtain.

First, of course, he was priest, confessor, and friend of the people who affectionately called him *"Père."* He used St. Thomas Church in Point-à-la-Hache as his base, and from there he served many missions in outlying areas. Traveling from one to another on a little launch named "St. Thomas," he fired his gun or rang a bell to let everyone know when he had arrived.

Fr. Girault gave Mother Katharine a memorable tour of his territory. The two of them dove into their work with abandon, unafraid of the mess and hard physical work involved in bringing God's Word and humane conditions to the poor on the fringes of society. One of Katharine's letters gives a glimpse into the hearts and spirits of these two missionaries:

In point of fact, it was 9 o'clock when we got into the launch. We were just about to start when the boy reported that there was no gasoline for the launch. The gasoline secured, we started. The water was high, and the wind was equally high; the little launch was going up and down violently, but we succeeded in boarding it. Theoretically, we were to have reached Jesuit Bend in about two hours and a half. Actually, it took four hours and a half, but we had our accidents "en route." There were two large vessels—one from South America, the other a European vessel, and they crossed each other in the Mississippi River which, you may imagine, is very wide at this point. This caused the waves to run high. The South American boat, when they saw the priest, flung out to us a great big bunch of bananas, and Father leaned over and with his pole tried to catch it when it fell into the river.... Just at this point, the boy called out, "The skiff's gone, Father! The skiff's gone!" And there about 100 rods away was the skiff that belonged to the launch, bobbing up and down on the waves more violently than we were.... We had to retrace our way and go after it. In the most tantalizing way that skiff would elude the pursuers. Father would dive after it with his pole, and almost have it, when off it would go again. At length, we neared it, and Father leaned over so far that I caught hold of his coat-tails. Mother Ignatius caught hold of the habit to my use, and Father kept on tugging. The skiff moved to the prow of the boat. Father jerked himself loose, extricating himself with determination to get that skiff, and rushed to the front of the launch. Etienne at the helm said, "Father, you dare not go there." Father apparently had a great respect for his pilot for he proceeded no farther, but giving me a pole said: "Here, take this pole, and help." I don't know how it happened, but presently we both fell down and rolled on top of each other in the bottom of the launch. I forgot to mention that in pulling about Father's portmanteau opened, and his medicines (of which he had a great variety) spilled out, and bottles and pills rolled up and down in the boat. He said he never traveled without his medicines. Bravo! We finally caught the skiff.[1]

On their return, Mother Ignatius recommended that the general council forbid Mother Katharine from traveling again with such an incompetent pilot on such an unreliable boat.

The travel was unusual, but what Katharine saw was unthinkable: extreme poverty everywhere. Schools were shacks. Students were enrolled in some cases for only one month per year. Teachers were scarce.

At Fr. Girault's request, Mother Katharine sent money to build a school at City Price. It was only the first of a string of twenty-four schools that would one day wind through rural Louisiana. Later, teachers educated at Xavier University would staff them.

In his letter to Mother Katharine of September 1920, Fr. Girault detailed some of the furnishings for the residence used by two young women from Xavier: seats and table from a boat, pail for a washbasin, his camping tent for draperies. His church school served about one hundred children, and he would not have wanted to begin with anyone but the Xavier team. Desks, blackboards, and other furnishings provided by the Sisters of the Blessed Sacrament made his school, poor as it was, one of the best in the area.[2]

The Ku Klux Klan

Not surprisingly, missions of the Sisters of the Blessed Sacrament came under attack from those who abhorred the thought of blacks and whites living and working together. Katharine had funded a church in Beaumont, Texas, and soon after the Sisters of the Blessed Sacrament established a convent and school there. In the early 1920s, members of the Ku Klux Klan posted a notice on the church door, threatening to dynamite the church if services for blacks did not stop.

At that time, Katharine wrote:

Mother F. Xavier & I are just returning from a more than two months' travel in the South. I have been visiting our Convents at Atlanta, Macon, Nashville, Montgomery, Biloxi, New Orleans, New Iberia, Beaumont, Washington.

We are arranging to open a new Mission at Lake Charles, La. It is between New Iberia and Beaumont. In this last place the Ku Klux [Klan] posted a notification to the Pastor that if he did not get out of Beaumont in a week, they would beat him, and tar and feather him. They had done this two weeks before to one White man and one German priest in Texas.

On the Beaumont church (Colored church, right next to our convent) they posted that if the Colored continued to worship there, they would dynamite the church.—This posting happened the day we left, & Mother M. Visitation sent me a special delivery to New Iberia telling me of it. You may be sure I was anxious, I telegraphed to the pastor that I would bear the expense of two watchmen to guard church, convent & rectory at night. The priest held his ground & so did the Sisters and the Congregation. Just go on ·s usual.[3]

She went on to tell of a black parishioner, father of a member of the Sisters of the Holy Family, who was seized, beaten, dragged behind a car, and then told to leave in two days. Providentially, a fierce thunderstorm brought the incident to a close when it ripped through town, destroying the Ku Klux Klan offices and leaving the mission buildings untouched.

Final Missionary Years

Mother Katharine was driven by her love of God and her desire to serve neglected and oppressed people of color who had been pushed to the fringes of society. The missions of the Sisters of the Blessed Sacrament spanned the country, and Katharine kept abreast of each one. She crisscrossed the country making visitations, attending to the needs of missions and the sisters who staffed them.

Every year she distributed the income she received from her inheritance. But as Bishop O'Connor had warned her when she chose religious life, even that was not enough. She would need "all [her] income, and ten times more, to make it accomplish its object partially."[4]

The need for additional funds was great, and Mother Katharine had ideas for securing new money for the missions. One proposal was forming an Auxiliary Society of the Sisters of the Blessed Sacrament. She began this work in 1928 and received support for it from Pope Pius XI.

Katharine hoped this organization would be a way to involve lay people who were interested in the missions and the work of the sisters but were unable to be directly involved. If all American Catholics contributed just one dollar per year, millions could be raised. The organization was turned over first to Mother Mercedes and later to Mother

Xavier. It did not raise millions, but Mother Katharine was grateful for the funds that were generated.

Katharine also tried to find ways to make the missions self-supporting, or at least less dependent on the order's money. Sometimes she approached bishops to see whether they could support missions in their dioceses. She also tried to cut down costs by turning boarding schools into day schools.

During these years other changes took place in the missions and schools. Some, like Xavier, expanded and needed new buildings. Land was purchased, and the new facility was opened in 1932. Many who saw Xavier commented on the beauty and excellence of the facilities.

In response to interest generated by the expansion, Mother Katharine gave her first interview to the press. Her students, children of God, deserved the best, she said, and the best is what they received. Xavier grew from a school offering elementary and "normal school" classes into a fine, accredited liberal arts college that today has a reputation for excellence in many fields, especially science.

Many black leaders have graduated from this university. For many years, more black graduates from Xavier entered medical school than from any other college or university in the United States. Xavier also has an outstanding school of pharmacy and offers master's degree programs in other areas of study. Since its beginnings, the School of Music has offered fully staged operas to the New Orleans area.

Some consider Xavier University the pinnacle of the work of Mother Katharine and the Sisters of the Blessed Sacrament. It is certainly the largest and most visible of their establishments, and it affects the lives of many beyond its campus. Still, looking with St. Katharine's eyes, perhaps the unsung sisters serving the disenfranchised in run-down American neighborhoods or poor South American countries add equally to the glory of the order.

Around the time that Xavier was expanding, other outreaches such as those in Boston changed location, and new missions were opened. The demands on Mother Katharine were great, and she embraced them with enthusiasm and intensity. By 1935, the Sisters of the Blessed Sacrament were supporting thirty-four missions. Even Mother Katharine could not physically keep up with them, though she tried.

In 1935 she made a staggering number of visitations, crisscrossing the country. Katharine always took a personal interest in members of the order. When she visited the missions she assumed work duties, giving the sisters time off.

She often traveled as well to nurse sick members of her order, preparing them special food to speed their recovery. This particular year she was concerned about a former superior who was having mental problems. Katharine visited her and accompanied her to a number of hospitals, securing the care of specialists.

The rigors of travel, the strain of concern for the missions and for her own sisters, and her penitential life eventually became too much for Katharine. Though she had had a small heart attack earlier in the year and dizzy spells, Mother Katharine was reluctant to slow her pace. While in Santa Fe she received word that the former superior who was ill was not responding to treatment. Katharine decided to go to Lamy, New Mexico, to meet her and then accompany her to Chicago.

All the while, Mother Katharine's own heart was wearing out. The driver who took her to Lamy noticed that she did not seem herself, but no one knew what loomed ahead.

After arriving in Chicago, she left the sister in the care of the sisters of St. Elizabeth's Convent. Then she and Mother Mary of the Visitation traveled to South Dakota, where a priest at one of their missions was forming a religious community for Native American women dedicated to doing similar work. He wanted the new community to be trained by the Sisters of the Blessed Sacrament, much as the Sisters of Mercy had guided Mother Katharine in her early days. Katharine was of course interested in the new work.

Still not feeling well, Katharine continued to worry about the sister in Chicago. She traveled there, brought her back to the next city of visitation—St. Louis—and settled her in St. Vincent's Sanitarium. Next Katharine was to return to Chicago. She made one last visit to the sister at St. Vincent's.

While there, Mother Katharine suffered a major heart attack. She remained at the sanitarium for two days and then, accompanied by a nurse, traveled back home. Her Jewish doctor, Max Herman, met her and admitted her to St. Joseph's Hospital, where she stayed until December 7.

Dr. Herman wasted no words. If Mother Katharine wanted to increase her chances of longevity, she would have to change her lifestyle radically. No more traveling across the country or taking care of details from the motherhouse. She needed complete rest. Mother Katharine accepted his diagnosis and returned home to begin another phase of her long life.

❧ EIGHT ❧

Life of Quiet Prayer

When Katharine Drexel first felt called to the religious life, she had been attracted to contemplative orders. She imagined herself free of the responsibilities that came with her position and inheritance, free to devote her life to prayer and adoration of the Lord, especially in the Eucharist. But Katharine had relinquished that dream and founded a missionary order instead. She had led an extremely active life that was sustained by prayer, the prayer of a contemplative in the world.

Now all that had changed. For the last years of her life she would live the prayer of quiet that she had desired in her youth.

A Graceful Change

After her heart attack, Katharine returned to the motherhouse and lived on the second floor in the infirmary. Mother M. Mercedes took over the administrative duties. Suddenly, but with grace and quiet submission to God's will, Mother Katharine made the transition from being a decision maker and traveling director of the order and its far-flung missions to being a contemplative who rarely made a trip downstairs.

In 1936, after Katharine suffered another minor heart attack, Louise Morrell hired a nurse to be with her during the day. Sisters stayed with her through the night.

A general chapter was held in 1937, and Mother M. Mercedes was elected the second superior general. During the following years, Mother Katharine was kept informed of the activities of the order. The sisters respected her knowledge, wisdom, and holiness, and those who had assumed her responsibilities solicited her advice. She was included in the life of the Sisters of the Blessed Sacrament in every way possible.

Mother Mercedes led the congregation for only a short while before being stricken with cancer. When she died in April 1940, Mother Katharine lost a dear friend who had been with her from the order's beginning. In June, Mother Mary of the Visitation was elected new superior general. She would oversee the great jubilee celebrations.

Jubilee

Always one to avoid publicity, Mother Katharine did not expect the recognition that came during her jubilee year. Beginning in 1939, colleges and universities contacted her, wanting to bestow honorary degrees. The first letter came from Bishop Joseph Corrigan, rector of Catholic University, who wanted her to receive their first honorary degree given to a woman. She accepted because she thought that "this declaration on the part of the Catholic University of America in esteem for work among the Colored and Indian People of the United States will give an added impetus and encouragement to this work."[1]

Three other degrees were awarded during her jubilee year, 1941. Duquesne bestowed an honorary Doctor of Pedagogy, and Emmanuel College of Boston gave her their first honorary degree, a Doctor of Humane Letters. St. Joseph's College, Philadelphia, bestowed the Doctor of Laws Degree on both Mother Katharine and her sister, Louise Morrell.

The year 1941 marked not only Mother Katharine's jubilee but also that of her order. A small celebration was held on February 12, the day Katharine had both taken her vows and been appointed superior of the new order. A larger celebration was held on April 18, 19, and 20 of that year. One day was designated for priests, another for religious, and one for lay people.

Priests, bishops, and cardinals; alumni, young students from her missions and older students from Xavier University; Native Americans, blacks, and whites all filled the grounds and the chapel. Native Americans performed dances, and prayer ties were offered. Choirs and glee clubs sang, and Xavier University's music department performed a scene from the opera *Carmen*. Such diversity gave testimony to the good work Mother Katharine and the Sisters of the Blessed Sacrament had accomplished.

Katharine appreciated the richness of the races to whom she had devoted her life. But even more, she cherished the unity found only in recognizing all people as children of God, gathered around the Eucharistic table. What joy must have filled her heart as she watched the long line of people from across cultures and across the country, young and old, process up the chapel's aisle to receive Holy Communion! Truly, that must have been a glimpse of the vision she had long held in her heart.

Her remaining years were spent in prayer and adoration of the Blessed Sacrament. While she was able, she walked or was wheeled in her chair to a small mezzanine that had been built for her by Colonel Morrell years before. The little balcony juts out above the sanctuary in the main chapel. There she could attend Mass or spend time before the Blessed Sacrament.

In 1943, when she was seriously ill, Cardinal Dennis Dougherty gave permission for Mass to be said daily in her room. The small wooden altar that had been in the convent of the Sisters of the Sacred Heart where she and her two sisters had made their First Communion, and that later had been at the Drexel home, was brought to her room. Every day she was able to receive her Lord in the Eucharist.

During these years Katharine made notes on scraps of paper or in little notebooks. On some she made lists of prayers to be said and intentions to be remembered. On others she wrote reflections or meditations. Her nights as well as her days were filled with prayer. When she could not sleep she prayed the rosary over and over again. Her night nurse, one of the sisters, would join with her.

Louise Morrell visited once a week, often bringing a basket of treats to share. She and Mother Katharine talked and made decisions about the dispersal of their inheritance. The Catholic Interracial Group in New York was often the recipient of funds, and the two sisters kept in touch with its leader, Fr. LaFarge, S.J. They also wrote letters to news media and politicians when issues of discrimination came to their attention.

Katharine was sensitive to the inordinate amount of publicity given to criminals' race if they were black. She advised her sisters across the country to look for racism in newspapers and respond when they saw it. Even from the infirmary, Mother Katharine's heart was focused on helping those she had set out to serve so many years before.

Without warning, on November 5, 1943, Louise died of a cerebral hemorrhage. Mother Katharine could not believe her beloved little sister had been snatched so suddenly from her. She profoundly missed their weekly visits, their shared passion for racial equality, and their remembrances of childhood days.

Of all the Francis Drexel family, Katharine alone was left. She grieved, but as always she embraced the pain life brought, and in doing so found a way to serve God's will.

In the midst of her routine of prayer, Mother Katharine received visitors from her congregation. They kept her informed of their missionary efforts. As years passed and she weakened, visitations were restricted. Still she thought of others. She asked her nurse whether the children were warm and had blankets like her own.

A story is told of Mother Katharine gazing for a long while at one place on the ceiling. After watching it for a while, she asked the sister attending her whether she had seen "them." When the nurse asked, "Seen what?" Mother Katharine replied that she had seen thousands of children walking by. The sister on duty thought perhaps Mother had seen a vision of all the children who had been brought to the Church through the efforts of the Sisters of the Blessed Sacrament.[2]

Besides her concern for others, especially the children, Katharine also thought about her death. She prayed for grace to meet it with faith and courage. On February 20, 1955, she became ill with pneumonia, and though she recovered, her physician said she still had a heart murmur.

On the evening of March 2, Mother Katharine's breathing became rapid and labored after a coughing spell. The symptoms were relieved by an oxygen tent, and she was well enough to eat breakfast the next morning. However, breathing soon became a struggle.

The sisters were called and knelt in her room, surrounding her with prayer. The chaplain and her physician were also in her room. At 9:05 A.M., March 3, 1955, her prayers answered, Mother Katharine met death with grace, passing into eternal life peacefully and without struggle.

Road to Sainthood

As was their custom, the Sisters of the Blessed Sacrament brought Katharine Drexel's body to the motherhouse chapel. For two days, lines of mourners filed by. Just as clergy, religious, and lay people had come to celebrate her jubilee, they came again to say good-bye to their friend and benefactress.

Others who braved the cold, wet weather had only heard of her story. Already many were referring to her as a saint. Some parents lifted their children so they could later say they had looked upon a saint. Sisters standing at the head and foot of the casket touched religious articles to her body for those who asked. As people continued to arrive, police were needed to keep traffic flowing.

Mother Katharine's funeral was held in the Cathedral of Sts. Peter and Paul in Philadelphia. Large as it is, it was unable to hold the throngs of people who gathered there, and many people spilled out into the street. Archbishop Edwin O'Hara said the Mass, assisted by more than 250 bishops, priests, and brothers.

Native Americans, blacks, and whites carried her body out of the cathedral together. The funeral procession wound through the grounds of Eden Hall, where sisters stood holding candles and children sang and recited the rosary. The procession ended at the mother-house, where Mother Katharine was laid to rest in a crypt built for her beneath the chapel.

Just nine years after her death, on February 27, 1964, the process for beatification was begun, introduced in Rome by then Archbishop John Krol of Philadelphia. Her writings were approved by the Congregation for the Causes of the Saints in 1973, and in 1987 Mother Katharine was declared Venerable. A miracle attributable to her intercession was needed in order to have her declared Blessed.

One was found in the healing of Robert Gutherman, a young boy from Bensalem, Pennsylvania. Part of a large Catholic family, he and his brothers often served Mass in the motherhouse chapel. In 1974 Robert, then fourteen, developed a severe ear infection that destroyed his eardrum and two of the three small bones of his inner ear. Doctors operated and said he would always be deaf in that ear.

Nevertheless, the Sisters of the Blessed Sacrament, Robert, and his family prayed through the intercession of Katharine Drexel for a cure. Two weeks after the surgery, Robert's eardrum had regenerated, and he could hear normally again. Doctors had no medical explanation. On November 20, 1988, Katharine Drexel was declared Blessed.

A second miracle required for Katharine to be declared "saint" also involved the restoration of hearing. Amanda Wall was born in 1992 in Bucks County, Pennsylvania. Her mother noticed that Amy did not react to loud noises or cry as other babies did in the nursery.

When the same behavior persisted at home, she sought medical counsel. Amy was diagnosed with nerve deafness in both ears. In November 1993, a television special about Blessed Katharine caught Mrs. Wall's attention. She watched and learned about Robert Gutherman's cure.

Encouraged, she and her family began praying that they would be able to communicate with Amy. Amy's brother, who was preparing to receive his First Communion, wanted to pray for a miracle instead. In March 1994, his prayer was answered when Amy's preschool teacher noticed a marked change in the child's behavior. Tests later that month showed that Amy had normal hearing in both ears. After a number of follow-up tests and a review by a medical board could show no medical reason for Amy's cure, it was classified as a true miracle attributed to the intercession of Blessed Katharine Drexel.

On October 1, 2000, Katharine Drexel was officially recognized as a saint of the Roman Catholic Church. Many of her congregation; Robert Gutherman, Amy Wall, and their families; alumni of schools her order had established; and many more whose lives had been touched by Mother Katharine's life gathered in Rome for the celebration. At the same ceremony Pope John Paul II also canonized a Spaniard, Maria Josefa of the Heart of Jesus; 120 Chinese martyrs; and Madre Josephine Bakhita of Italy and the Sudan.

Rain did not stop more than eighty thousand people from filling St. Peter's Square. How fitting it was to celebrate her canonization with other new saints and people of many races. Katharine would have enjoyed the diversity of the pilgrims, their songs, and their dress. The Mass incorporated prayers, dances, and music of many cultures, including that of Native Americans and blacks. The day celebrated not only St. Katharine Drexel but the wide embrace of the Catholic Church and the unity experienced in the Eucharist.

St. Katharine considered herself an instrument of the Church. Her strength and direction came from her prayer and experience of God mediated through the Church, its ministers, and its sacraments. Her work, and that of the Sisters of the Blessed Sacrament, was done for love of God in the name of the Church. She loved its affirmation of the communion of saints and the Mystical Body of Christ. She felt strongly a connection with the great missionaries and the faithful of all ages, past, present, and to come.

Those who knew Katharine say she always sat on the edge of her chair intently listening to anyone who spoke to her. Now a member of the communion of saints, she is just as eager to listen and to intercede for any who seek her help. St. Katharine Drexel's feast is celebrated on March 3. Through her canonization, she now belongs to all people, an example of the holiness to which everyone is called.

❧ NINE ❧

Katharine Drexel's Spirituality

St. Katharine's spirituality was rooted in two great loves. The first and primary one was her passionate love of God. From that grew the second, love of others, particularly the poor and forgotten. Like the two great commandments that sum up God's will for all people, these loves guided her life. They fueled both her contemplative prayer and the active work in the world that was sustained by it.

Contemplative

Katharine was a natural contemplative, experiencing God in her soul's depths. She moved easily from appreciating the moment to knowing God's presence in it. She often saw in the world around her a metaphor for relationship with God. In many letters written to sisters at the motherhouse, she shifts from describing what she sees to sharing some part of her experience or spiritual insight and then, just as quickly, she returns to her narrative.

Once while traveling by train between missions, she wrote of flowers in a small box at her feet. Someone had sprinkled them with water in the morning, and Katharine let the water be absorbed a bit before closing them in. When she opened the box to look and enjoy the fragrance, she noticed that one bunch of violets placed alone in a corner had faded, while violets nestled under the flaming red tulips were still fresh and lovely.

As Thoreau said, it isn't what we look at that matters, but what we see. Wherever she looked, Katharine saw divine love. The love of Jesus, she wrote, makes "humiliation sweet."

Is it not also true that the flaming love of Jesus and the red Precious Blood must also cover us before we can bring forth in God's garden of our hearts, the humble, sweet, fresh, little violets of humility so pleasing to the Beloved. We must not forget humility is God's gift to us and we must ask for it and do our little best when an opportunity comes to bring forth the hidden flower.[1]

Her natural sense of prayer was in part an inheritance from her parents. Francis and Emma Drexel were deeply aware of the sacrament of matrimony, lived out day by day. Mr. Drexel's letter written to his wife on New Year's Day 1863 shows an understanding of the sacramentality of matrimony—God using husband, wife, and their daily lives to bring them to holiness and to make them more perfect in their reflection of God:

Many various blessings have been conferred upon us the time we have been united—A special Providence it has been that has brought us together and if we operate according to its designs it will be the means of amending much in us that needs correction. A similarity in feeling and disposition, unless regulated by mutual love and forbearance, does not in general produce perfect concord—What each of us offends in, we are less likely to forgive in the other—Mutual forbearance is necessary for us both.... We have received many and various blessings. Let us not be forgetful of them but in time to come may we show by our punctuality in approaching the Blessed Sacrament and the attention and devotion that we manifest in preparing for it, that we appreciate the means of salvation which have been designed to sustain our spiritual life. May our hearts be continually directed toward Him who suffered and died for us and gave His Flesh for our life— When tempted let us instantly call on our Blessed Mother—She is our friend and will help us.... In conclusion, my dear, dear one, let me wish you a happy New Year indeed, a strength to bear all the little trials that may befall you. May your warm, tender, and loving heart beat yet more tenderly toward your own loving and affectionate husband pardoning him his faults and sustaining him in his trials and thus make home a heaven here below.[2]

The expectation of meeting God in married life and being transformed by the encounter reflects an understanding that is often overlooked. The partners gaze not only on one another, but together they look to God. Children growing up in such an atmosphere cannot help but absorb the unspoken lessons: God is with us. God is part of everyday affairs. God listens and transforms. When we falter, Mary, too, is our help.

As foundress of a new order, Katharine retained that refreshing sense of God's imminence and was comfortable having conversations with her Lord. A Sister of the Blessed Sacrament remembers her surprise as a postulant when Mother Katharine departed from formal prayers and spoke to God from her heart:

She came into chapel this one afternoon before Vespers and she put her head down on her stall. Then she picked it up and she held her hands out, she came down and said, "O Lord, grant that we may love you the way you deserve to be loved." I was a postulant. I was so startled by the whole thing I looked around to see what everybody else's reaction was. Nobody even reacted.... The night prayers she said were also from her heart. She added what she wanted to add.... Every night it was customary for us to mention every single mission and if some mission needed something she would always stop and say, "Now Lord, give San Jose this," or "Make sure that Xavier gets this."[3]

Blessed Sacrament

Katharine desired quiet union with God and eternal life lived as close to the Lord as possible. Her thirst for God intensified through the years, and her longing to be in God's presence manifested itself in devotion to Jesus in the Blessed Sacrament. Early in her search for a religious community she was drawn to contemplative orders that allowed frequent reception of the Sacrament.

As a child, she had craved reception of the Eucharist long before the privilege was hers. From early visits before the tabernacle made with her mother, to her final years when she received permission for Mass to be said in her room, Katharine drew strength and peace from the Blessed Sacrament.

She knew the unitive effect of becoming one with Jesus each time she received the Host. Through the grace of the Eucharist she was connected with others who also were drawn into that mystical union through the Sacrament. She wrote of that reality in a letter to Louise and Ned Morrell when they were away on their honeymoon.

On the 29th we had a sweet, quiet little Mass celebrated (at F.A. Drexel memorial altar in the Cathedral) by His Grace at seven. It was happiness for us to feel all—the dear ones who have gone before us to God—and your dearest Sister & Brother—to feel that no distance in heaven or on earth could separate us when our Lord in the Blessed Sacrament connected us, united us all together.[4]

Union with Jesus in the Eucharist, and through him to all others, was central to Mother Katharine's spirituality. In Jesus, she and her sisters were united not only to one another but also to those they served.

Unity was a theme that ran through much of her correspondence. In a letter to young novices in Pittsburgh awaiting her summons to join her at San Michel, Mother Katharine shared that vision. These insights were included in "Counsels and Maxims," which was assembled later for the community's use.

In that very first letter which the young Mother Foundress addressed to her flock, she refers for the first time to the necessity of union in all things. She told them it was Christ's special prayer and precept when He first gave Himself to mankind in the Blessed Sacrament in the First Holy Communion of the chosen Twelve Apostles: "Abide in Me, and I in you.... I am the Vine, you the branches ..." She impressed upon them the importance of taking to heart Our Lord's injunction: "If we abide in the Vine we shall indeed be one," she concluded, "and I should write the word ONE in capitals, for surely by abiding in our Jesus, Who is our All, we shall be united in Him in charity for one another and thus bring forth much fruit in souls."[5]

Throughout her years as a Sister of the Blessed Sacrament, building a church or chapel where the Eucharist could be shared was an essential part of every mission. She wanted to bring as many souls as possible to the Eucharistic table. Her desire to share this miraculous gift with others, especially the poor, was the force that propelled her to found missions across the country.

To those forgotten people and places she wanted to bring opportunities for education and for acquiring skills that would provide a livelihood. But most of all, she wanted to bring God's presence in the Eucharist.

Poverty

Embracing poverty was another hallmark of Katharine's spirituality. She was a Third Order Franciscan, and much like St. Francis of Assisi, she left behind a life of wealth and privilege for the joy of serving "Lady Poverty." Jesus' words in Matthew 19:21 were pivotal in her spiritual journey: "If you would be perfect, go, sell what you possess and give to the poor, and you will have treasure in heaven; and come, follow me".

Katharine desired perfection. She wanted to give herself completely to God and, like Francis, to follow Jesus as closely as she could: "I have meditated on the Nativity and looked upon the poverty of our Lord in the stable and thought He chose this portion for Himself because poverty was the most honorable to God and the most beneficial to mankind."[6]

When Katharine was making plans to establish her order, Bishop O'Connor suggested that each year she lay aside a certain amount of her inheritance, creating a trust that would fund the sisters and their work. After prayerfully considering the idea, she decided not to do it. She did not want her order to begin with an advantage other orders did not have: wealth. She chose poverty instead. Over the years, her yearly income was spent to sustain the missions and do the work of the order.

A Sister of the Blessed Sacrament who was Katharine's night nurse from 1951 to 1953 remembers the importance the saint placed on trusting in God's care for all needs. The foundress's instructions, passed through the novice mistress to new postulants, was "to have a deep faith, no matter what happens, to believe that God was there ... good can come out of it. 'Trust in Divine Providence.' That is what St. Katharine said. 'Trust in Divine Providence.'"[7]

Neither was St. Katharine interested in changing her father's will, as some suggested she do. Surely, he would have wanted to support his daughter's foundation, they argued. But she would not change it.

God would provide, she insisted: "I cannot see that God would not be more glorified by making the new order share the fate of all the others who have showed such self-sacrifice in the work. God give us their evangelical spirit of poverty and detachment!"[8]

Personally, she lived evangelical poverty. Her abrupt change from being a woman of wealth to being a poor postulant was noted by one of the Sisters of Mercy: "Her spirit of poverty was evidenced at recreation where we would see her scrupulously mending her clothes, darning her stockings.... In fact she wasted nothing."[9]

To give testimony to her practice of keeping items in service long beyond their usual period of utility, a variety of articles are kept in the archives of the order. One is a habit covered with patches and carefully darned holes, mended with small, even stitches. Her shoes are another. She repaired them herself when the cobbler pronounced them beyond salvaging.

Every penny saved was used to support a needy child, school, or mission. Visiting classrooms, she often took new pencils and traded with children for their old, worn-out ones. She used these until they were stubs, writing prayers and reflections on scraps of paper or used envelopes she had unfolded.

Katharine practiced self-denial, dispensing with what she felt was unnecessary. She ate little and sought no variety in her food. The sisters were often concerned that she did not eat enough to maintain her health, and occasionally they enlisted the help of Archbishop Ryan. While she would not respond to their pleas, when he told her to allow herself more food, she obeyed the voice of the Church through him.

Joy and Humility

Those who knew Katharine remarked often on her joy and humility. Fr. John LaFarge, who spoke often with Mother Katharine about racial justice issues, remembered her "light and joyous incisiveness," and that even at "eighty and then some she still kept a glimmer of the almost mischievous glee with which she recalled her early rides through the deserts and prairies of the West."[10]

Her joy and unassuming nature endeared her to those she met. "No one was more approachable, no one simpler in her tastes or more unpretentious in manner.... The general picture she presented ... is a picture of joy. For all the toil, the journeyings, the difficulties, the hardships of the way, she abounded in joy."[11]

Fr. Berard Haile, one of the Franciscans who came to St. Michael's in Arizona in 1900, remembered that she was "a very agreeable woman":

In fact, she seemed to be simply a sister among her sisters, and she had to be pointed out to us as the superior of the community.... She did the same work as the other sisters and she was happy and jolly with them all the time.... Very often I met the Mother Superior on her knees scrubbing the porch and sweeping the rooms.[12]

Contemplative in Action

Katharine was a contemplative in the world, a woman of quiet prayer, yes, but also a woman of action. In her life, artificial boundaries between prayer and action vanished as they should. Prayer takes different forms, but God is present both in the kitchen and the church.

> Lord, where do You dwell? He dwells in the little opportunities which arise of doing well or suffering well. He dwells in the humble homes as in His consecrated hosts and beneath the appearance of chance annoyances, of disagreeable illnesses, of unprofitable work, of sacrifices claimed, of meritorious obedience.... And my life passes close to these His dwellings and my days meet them at each moment.[13]

Katharine's prayer life fueled her desire to serve. The deeper her relationship with the Holy One, the more she wanted to share God with those who had not heard the gospel. While evangelizing was her primary goal, she also wanted to alleviate physical suffering. Her mother's example had taught Katharine well, and she heeded her Master's words: "Whatsoever you do to the least of these, you do to me" (see Mt 25:40).

Her life of contemplation and action is a model for all today. Christ has given all a share in his redemptive work, as well as the means to nourish themselves by sinking roots into divine life. The challenges of living as a Christian in the midst of a world indifferent or increasingly hostile to the faith cannot be met relying on human strength alone.

In retreat notes Katharine wrote: "Union with God alone gives *life* and abundance of *life*.... No creature gives light. *We are not* sufficient in ourselves. My God! How often I have experienced this!"[14]

Though she died several years before Blessed Pope John XXIII became pope, Katharine's life exemplified words from his encyclical *Mater et Magistra:*

> Wherever men are to be found who are in want of food and drink, of clothing, housing, medicine, work, education, the means necessary for leading a truly human life, wherever there are men racked by misfortune or illness, men suffering exile or imprisonment, Christian Charity should go in search of them and find them out, comfort them with devoted care and give them the helps that will relieve their needs. This obligation binds first and foremost the more affluent individuals and nations.[15]

In the missions of the Sisters of the Blessed Sacrament, Katharine made sure that the school provided such helps.

In a letter she shared her joy at seeing the work and study being done by students at St. Catherine's.

> The work of the boys in a building commenced last year is a wonder. It is all pupil labor with a competent contractor to show the boys how to work.... One day I was watching them work. They were up to the roof.... The big boys were laying the adobe.

They had boards on a slant which made a sort of runway and the little boys had small wheelbarrows and were running them up this runway with two adobe bricks at a time.... It was certainly well managed. We started First Year High School at Santa Fe and you will wonder why. Well, because New Mexico has passed a law that nurses cannot be certified unless they have one year High School training, and our Indian girls find it a splendid means of livelihood.... I am anxious always in these schools to enable the children to make a livelihood.[16]

Social Justice

St. Katharine's efforts for social justice included but did not stop at establishing a system of schools from elementary to university level for black and Native Americans. Decades before the Civil Rights movement, she along with Louise Morrell actively worked to bring issues of racial justice to the fore. They supported Fr. John LaFarge and the Catholic Interracial Council, which eventually consolidated with other groups and became the National Catholic Conference for Interracial Justice.

Fr. LaFarge appreciated not only the monetary support but also Katharine's personal involvement in racial justice issues. He wrote: "Where human rights were concerned, Mother Katharine rose to the challenge."[17] She involved the sisters socially and politically by encouraging them to write letters: to newspaper editors about unfair publicity for crimes committed by blacks, and to congressmen and President Roosevelt in support of the antilynching bill.

Katharine funded an NAACP investigation of racism in the South and became involved in protesting unfair labor conditions for black workers in the Mississippi Flood Control Project. When the Scottsboro Boys were unjustly accused of raping two white women, she became involved in the committee set up to help build a defense fund.

Her efforts helped focus the attention of the American Catholic Church on the problem of racism. She did this in part by her approach to combating the problem. Hers was not social work. It was the Church's work. She saw every person as a brother or sister in Christ, deserving equal opportunity to hear the gospel and to enjoy quality education.

In this regard, Mother Anna Dengel, foundress of the Medical Mission Sisters, was quoted by Fr. LaFarge in an article in the August 1957 *Interracial Review.* "To my mind," she insisted, "Mother Katharine saved the reputation of the United States as regards the racial question."[18]

Serious justice issues confront today's world. Environmental, economic, political, and racial issues call for action informed by faith. Katharine is a model for our day: one who was not afraid to get in the thick of controversy when necessary, who was willing to work within the system when necessary, and who had the humility to learn from others and from her experiences.

Daughter of the Church

Katharine grew up in a family deeply committed to the Catholic Church, and her spirituality was rooted in her faith. Sr. Consuela Duffy wrote: "She was conscious always that she was working for the Church under the direction of Church authorities, that she was an instrument of the Church."[19]

During the jubilee celebration Mother Katharine told the sisters:

I want to say that I thank God I am a child of the Church. I thank God it was my privilege to meet many of the great missionaries of the Church and to have had the prayers of those great missionaries like Monsignor Stephen and Bishop Marty.... I saw them in their agony. I saw them in their agony, those great souls! I thank God He gave me the grace to see their lives. They are a part of the Church of God, and I thank God like the great St. Theresa that I, too, am a child of the Church.[20]

Katharine rejoiced in being a member of the Church that embraced famous saints as well as the unknown faithful servants of God. She longed to extend that membership to all. The strength and wisdom, the love and humility, that were the fruit of her prayer were spent on continuing Jesus' work through the Church. And when her body grew old and weak, she continued to be a conduit of God's grace, resting in the divine presence.

Katharine's spirituality is one of unity in God mediated through the Church. While every person has a unique role in bringing about the kingdom of God, each one can draw strength from the Blessed Sacrament. St. Katharine envisioned a human family free of racial prejudices and the discrimination engendered by them, gathering at the Eucharistic table and going out into the world to let God's redemptive grace flow through them, transforming creation.

It is a vision, a way of prayer, that offers hope for a world that still groans with pain born of hate and division. It is a vision of poverty that challenges consumerism and calls people to rethink their use of resources and their stewardship of the earth. St. Katharine Drexel's spirituality calls all to a more intentional existence as members of both the human family and the family of God.

Prayers and Admonitions of
St. Katharine Drexel

Oh my God, I love You above all things with my whole heart and soul, and for Your sake I love my neighbor as myself for the love of You. Mercifully grant that, having loved You on earth, I may love and enjoy You in Heaven.[1]

O divine Spirit, I wish to be before You as a light feather, so that Your Breath may carry me where You will.[2]

O dearest Jesus, teach me to be generous—make me generous to give and not to count the cost. Grant, I beseech You, oh grant that my heart wholly united to You may be closed to my enemies, dead to myself and to the world, ever open to You, breathing You alone, above all things loving You.[3]

My dear Jesus, through Your sacred wounds and agonizing death, grant me the grace to expire in Your love and friendship. O Sacred Heart of Jesus, I believe in Your love for me. O Jesus, Divine Savior, grant that I be no longer deaf to Your heavenly call but prompt and diligent in accomplishing Your Will. Make me Yours at any cost. Give me courage to overcome every obstacle in Your holy service. Draw me continually, dearest Jesus, to closer union with You.[4]

Growth must be gradual to be enduring.[5]

Here are little things, without a doubt, but God knows if these little things have not their price and if the love of God with which they are done is not truly a great love.[6]

Teach children with joy. They will be attracted by joy to the source of all joy, the Heart of Jesus.[7]

If then we wish to serve God and love our neighbor well, we must manifest our joy in the service we render to Him and to them—*servite in laetitia*. Oh, let us do this and not change the nature of things. God is Joy; true devotion is joy; the cross is the condition of solid joy. Let us open wide our hearts. It is Joy which invites us. Press forward and fear nothing.[8]

Keep Him so near to you that you will not have more than a step to take to find yourself with Him and so that a mere whisper of His may be heard in your heart. He whispers, "Come," for He will not tell you to go—alone. No, He beckons you to come with Him.[9]

You must forget self to remember Our Lord.[10]

I love to think how small the little foot of Our Lord was on that first Christmas. A little foot does not make big strides; it can only take little steps. In imitating the divine Babe, let us place ours in His footsteps, then we shall, with God's grace, grow into the bigger footsteps and make greater strides. If we are faithful in little, we will obtain grace for the big.[11]

Let us often contemplate Jesus our Lord on His last journey. He bids me follow Him. There is no other way to heaven. No one's face is toward heaven when it is not toward Calvary.[12]

The patient and humble endurance of the cross—whatever nature it may be—is the highest work we have to do.[13]

The one utility of the creature is this alone: to do God's will, even if He wishes you to be absolutely idle. To place your happiness in having a great deal to do when you are not able to do it is a false happiness, not according to the heart of God. All your happiness must be in serving God according to His will. Impossible then to be out of place, for the only thing out of place is that which is outside of God's will.[14]

God has made Himself to you Father, Brother, Spouse. God always loves more truly, more ardently than He is loved. Love Him and He holds your love worthy. Love not in word, but in work.[15]

I looked up in wonder at God's wonderful ways and thought how little we imagine what may be the result of listening and acting on a desire He puts into the heart. If He puts it into the heart, He will bless it, if we try to act upon it, and great will be the effect before God. It will be a success before God, even if it be not so to our weak understanding. For God means that which He breathes into the soul should bring forth fruit to eternal life.[16]

Sisters of the Blessed Sacrament Today

The order founded by St. Katharine is still serving God in the poor and marginalized people of the world, with an emphasis on education, social justice, and evangelization. More than 220 sisters live in forty-three convents across the United States. Education remains an important part of their ministry, with S.B.S. sisters involved at elementary through university levels. Their schools span the country from St. Michael's in Arizona to St. Ignatius in Philadelphia to Xavier University in New Orleans.

Sisters of the Blessed Sacrament are also involved in social services, pastoral care, nursing, administration, and social justice work. They continually discern responses to today's global challenges. In the early 1980s the order extended its reach to include a Haitian mission where economic development and social services are a major focus. Following Katharine's example, the sisters preach by actions as well as with words.

In 1981 the order appointed a director of social justice to educate herself and the sisters about world issues and responses to them. Through her, the order supports HONOR, an advocacy group for Native Americans, and Fund for an Open Society, a Philadelphia-based group that works toward integrating neighborhoods. A major part of the director's time is spent with ICCR (Interfaith Center on Corporate Responsibility).

The education process extends to the community at large as they look to the future, including stewardship of their land holdings. Recently some of the community members spoke with Thomas Berry, an eminent cultural historian and author who addresses the ecological issues of our day. Together they hope to develop long-term land use directives.

All activity is rooted in community life and prayer, including daily Mass and Eucharist. The sisters' response to the world grows, as Katharine's did, out of love for God and love for God's people, especially the poor and disenfranchised.

For more information about the Sisters of the Blessed Sacrament, visit their website at www.katharinedrexel.org.

❧ NOTES ❧

Abbreviations

ASBS   Archives of the Sisters of the Blessed Sacrament
MKDLS   Mother M. Katharine Drexel's Letters to Sisters
O An   Original Annals of the Sisters of the Blessed Sacrament
ODC   O'Connor-Drexel Correspondence
SBS An   Annals of the Sisters of the Blessed Sacrament

Introduction

1. Sr. Consuela Marie Duffy, S.B.S., *Katharine Drexel: A Biography* (Bensalem, Penn.: Mother Katharine Drexel Guild, Sisters of the Blessed Sacrament, 1966), 360.
2. Duffy, 397.

ONE
Roots

1. "Catherine" was her given name, although she had nicknames during her younger years and spelled her name "Katharine" later on.
2. Sr. M. Dolores Letterhouse, S.B.S., *The Francis A. Drexel Family* (privately published, 1939), 11.

TWO
Early Years

1. Letterhouse, 44.
2. Katie Drexel Letters, ASBS.
3. Katie Drexel Letters, ASBS.
4. Duffy, 31.
5. Memoir of Mother M. Katharine Drexel, November 11, 1935, ASBS.
6. Katie Drexel Diary, Sunday, January 23, ASBS.
7. Katie Drexel Letters, ASBS.
8. Letterhouse, 77, quoting from Katie Drexel Letters, ASBS.
9. Duffy, 45.
10. Duffy, 59.
11. Duffy, 60.
12. Duffy, 62.
13. Duffy, 62.
14. Letterhouse, 89.
15. Letterhouse, 90.
16. O An, vol. 1, 35.

THREE
Eventful Years

1. ODC, May 28, 1878, ASBS.
2. January 10, 1879, quoted in Letterhouse, 155-56.
3. Duffy, 67.
4. Letterhouse, 185.
5. Duffy, 70.

6. ODC, May 21, 1883, ASBS.

7. ODC, May 26, 1883, ASBS.

8 ODC, August 5, 1883, ASBS.

9. ODC, September 8, 1883, ASBS.

10. ODC, On board the *Scythia,* ASBS.

11. ODC, October 25, 1883, ASBS.

12. ODC, January 27, 1884, ASBS.

13. ODC, Long Branch, Seacliff Villa, June, 1884, ASBS.

14. Letterhouse, 234.

FOUR

Discerning Her Vocation

1. ODC, August 1885, ASBS.

2. Katharine Drexel's "Diary of a Trip to Europe, 1886-87," ASBS [hereafter cited as "Europe"].

3. Europe, 1886-87, ASBS, quoting Gn 28:16.

4. Europe, 1886-87, ASBS.

5. Europe, 1886-87, ASBS.

6. Duffy, 100.

7. Letterhouse, 305.

8. ODC, March 5, 1887, ASBS.

9. This author uses the term "Lakota" rather than "Sioux," since the latter was actually a derogatory term used by Northern Great Lakes Tribes who drove the Lakota into the Great Plains.

10. Letterhouse, 334 (punctuation added for clarity).

11. Letterhouse, 344.

12. ODC, May 16, 1888, ASBS.

13. Duffy, 108.

14. ODC, November 26, 1888, ASBS.
15. ODC, November 30, 1888, ASBS.
16. ODC, December 15, 1888, ASBS.
17. Letterhouse, 344.
18. ODC, February 12, 1889, ASBS.
19. ODC, February 16, 1889, ASBS.
20. ODC, February 28, 1889, ASBS.
21. ODC, March 16, 1889, ASBS.
22. Duffy, 148.
23. ODC, March 19, 1889, ASBS.

FIVE

Years of Formation

1. ODC, April 6, 1889, ASBS.
2. Letterhouse, 358.
3. *Collection of articles compiled by SBS as bicentennial tribute...*, ASBS.
4. Letterhouse, 361.
5. Letterhouse, 359.
6. Duffy, 142.
7. ODC, May 12, 1889, ASBS.
8. Duffy, 160.
9. SBS An, 3/126.

SIX
Missions and the Rule

1. MKDLS, November 18, 1903, ASBS.
2. Duffy, 232.
3. Duffy, 360.
4. Duffy, 282.
5. Duffy, 292.
6. Duffy, 293.

SEVEN
The Work Continues

1. Rural School Correspondence, ASBS.
2. Rural School Correspondence, Letter to Mother Katharine from Fr. Jean Marie Girault de la Corgnais, September [date illegible], 1920, ASBS.
3. Writings of Mother Katharine, no. 2887 to Jo, ASBS.
4. ODC, February 16, 1889, ASBS.

EIGHT
Life of Quiet Prayer

1. Duffy, 365.
2. Duffy, 376.

NINE
Katharine Drexel's Spirituality

1. MKDLS, 1891–1900, vol. 1, 7, ASBS.
2. Letterhouse, 42.
3. Sr. Roberta Smith, S.B.S, in conversation with the author, March 5, 2001.
4. Letterhouse, 345.
5. "Counsels and Maxims," ASBS.
6. ODC, October 28, 1889, ASBS.
7. Sr. Inez Carney, S.B.S., in conversation with the author, March 1, 2001.
8. ODC, October 28, 1889, ASBS.
9. Duffy, 143.
10. Fr. John LaFarge, S.J., "America's Own Missionary: Mother M. Katharine Drexel (1858–1955)," condensed from *America* (March 19, 1955), ASBS. (See memorial volumes for additional obituaries.)
11. Duffy, 397.
12. Murray Bodo, O.F.M., ed., *Tales of an Endishodi: Father Berard Haile and the Navajos, 1900–1961* (Albuquerque, N.Mex.: University of New Mexico Press, 1998), as quoted in Pat McCloskey, O.F.M., "Mother Katharine Drexel and the Cincinnati Friars," *St. Anthony Messenger* (October 2000), 35.
13. Sr. Thomasita Daley, S.B.S., comp., *Praying with Mother Katharine Drexel*, 1986, ASBS, 18.
14. Duffy, 166-67.
15. Pope John XXIII, *Mater et Magistra*, as quoted in *Vatican Council II: The Conciliar and Post Conciliar Documents*, Austin Flannery, O.P., ed. (Northport, N.Y.: Costello, 1975), 776.

16. MKDLS, December 11, 1925, ASBS.
17. Fr. John LaFarge, *Interracial Review* (August 1957), ASBS.
18. LaFarge.
19. Duffy, 278.
20. Duffy, 358.

Prayers and Admonitions of St. Katharine Drexel

1. Daley, 9.
2. Daley, 13.
3. Daley, 15.
4. Daley, 28.
5. MKDLS 1891–1900, Thursday, 1894, ASBS.
6. "Counsels and Maxims," 14-15, ASBS.
7. "Counsels and Maxims," 20, ASBS; MKDLS 1891–1990, ASBS.
8. Mother M. Katharine Drexel, writings collected in *Reflections on Life in the Vine* [hereafter cited as *Vine*], compiled by Sisters of the Blessed Sacrament, 1983, 23.
9. Mother M. Katharine Drexel, writings collected in *Reflections on Religious Life*, compiled by Sisters of the Blessed Sacrament, 1983, 22.
10. Sr. Kathy Butler, comp., *Breadcrumbs*, ASBS; "Counsels and Maxims," ASBS.
11. *Vine*, 5.
12. *Vine*, 7.
13. *Vine*, 13.
14. *Reflections on Religious Life*, 30.
15. *Vine*, 15.
16. Duffy, 240.

Servant Publications
Charis Books

Meet the Saints Series

Cynthia Cavnar, *Meet Edith Stein*

Woodeene Koenig-Bricker, *Meet Dorothy Day*

George Kosicki, *Meet Saint Faustina*

Patricia Treece, *Meet Padre Pio*

Brother Leo Wollenweber, *Meet Solanus Casey*

Available at your local bookstore or wherever books are sold.